MacBrayne Steamers

Lochnevis departing Tarbert (for Islay) and Ardrishaig (for Oban and the north).

MacBrayne Steamers

by

Alistair Deayton

TEMPUS

Acknowledgements

The majority of the illustrations come from my own collection, built up over the past thirty-five years. Many were originally published by the Clyde River Steamer Club. Those, which I have obtained from other sources for this publication, are as follows

GEL	G.E. Langmuir collection, Glasgow Room, Mitchell Library, North St. Glasgow
QRC	Iain Quinn and Donald Robertson collections
AA	Alastair Aitken Collection
BP	Bert Pellegrom
CRSC	Clyde River Steamer Club slide archive and photo collection.
USNHS	United States Naval Historical Foundation, Washington, DC.

I am indebted to Duckworth and Langmuir's *West Highland Steamers* (4th edition, 1987) for most of the historical facts, also to various publications from the Clyde River Steamer Club. My thanks must also go to Iain Quinn and Robin Boyd who have checked my manuscript for errors and to Iain Hope for information on the first *Lochbuie*.

Front Cover: The cover of the Macbrayne timetable for 1935, showing *Lochfyne*, a route map and a MacBrayne bus.
Rear Cover: Lochnivar at Mallaig whilst on the Portree mail run in 1959.

First published 2002
Reprinted 2003, 2007

Tempus Publishing Limited
The Mill, Brimscombe Port,
Stroud, Gloucestershire, GL5 2QG

© Alistair Deayton, 2002

The right of Alistair Deayton to be identified as the Author
of this work has been asserted in accordance with the
Copyrights, Designs and Patents Act 1988.

British Library Cataloguing in Publication Data.
A catalogue record for this book is available from the British Library.

ISBN 978 0 7524 2362 3

Typesetting and origination by Tempus Publishing Limited

Contents

Map of the area covered by MacBrayne sailings from the 1934 timetable.

Introduction

For the past 150 years the name MacBrayne has been synonymous with shipping in the West Highlands and Islands of Scotland.

In 1851 David MacBrayne was a partner, along with David and Alexander Hutcheson, in the firm of David Hutcheson and Company.

In 1879 after the Hutcheson brothers had retired, David MacBrayne ran the company in his own name, On his retirement in 1905 his son David Hope MacBrayne founded David MacBrayne Ltd, assisted, for a time, by his brother, Lawrence MacBrayne.

In 1928 David MacBrayne (1928) Ltd was founded, jointly owned by Coast Lines Ltd and the London Midland & Scottish Railway. In 1934 this company was restyled David MacBrayne Ltd. In 1948 the LMSR was incorporated into British Railways. In January 1969 David MacBrayne Ltd was incorporated into the government-owned Scottish Transport Group and in July of that year the government purchased the Coast Lines share of the company. On 1 January 1973 David MacBrayne Ltd was subsumed into Caledonian MacBrayne Ltd.

MacBraynes were so much a part of the scene in the West Highlands that there was a popular parody of the psalm:

The Earth is the Lord's and all it contains, Except for the Western Isles, which belong to MacBraynes.

This book is an illustrated history of the steamers and motorships operated by MacBraynes from 1851 until the end of David MacBrayne Ltd operations in 1969 on the Clyde and 1972 in the West Highlands. MacBraynes vessels, which operated on inland lochs, are not covered in this volume. It is hoped that a later volume in this series will deal with Scottish Loch steamers.

The list of these vessels includes such notable steamers of their day as the paddle steamers *Columba* and *Iona* and the turbine *King George V*, which made the Staffa and Iona trip from Oban her own for almost forty years. There are also minor little-known cargo vessels like *Clydesdale* and *Lapwing* and of course, the 'wee red boats' which tendered *King George V* at Staffa and Iona and the mail boats at other small ports without piers.

Prior to 1851 G.&J. Burns and Messrs Thomson & McConnell had operated the services from Glasgow to the West Highlands jointly. The latter company transferred their services to G.&J. Burns in early 1851 and Burns to the newly formed firm of David Hutcheson & Co. in February of that year, the new company receiving eight paddle steamers and two track-boats (Crinan Canal passenger barges) from the previous operator. David MacBrayne, a nephew of the Burns brothers, was a partner in this company while David Hutcheson was chief clerk of G.&J. Burns.

Over the next six years a further four paddle steamers were built, including the fist *Iona*, and in 1857 Hutcheson took over the Glasgow & Lochfyne Steam Packet Company, including the *Mary Jane*, a steamer which was destined to last until 1931.

The early 1860s was the period of the American Civil War, and agents of the Confederate States purchased a number of fast British steamers, mainly paddle steamers, to run the blockade into the southern ports. Hutchesons sold the *Fingal*, which had been their first screw steamer, in 1861 after only four months service on the Glasgow to Stornoway service. She was converted to an ironclad and served in both the Confederate and Union Navies. The first *Iona* followed in October 1862, although she was sunk before leaving the Clyde in Gourock Bay after a collision. A second *Iona* was built in 1863 and sold at the close of the summer season, as was the two-year-old paddle steamer *Fairy*, but the former was sunk off Lundy.

A third *Iona* was built the following year to the same design, for the Glasgow to Ardrishaig service and she survived until scrapped in 1936.

The financial gain from the sale of these ships for blockade running enabled Hutchesons to invest in further new tonnage, including the *Gondolier* for the Caledonian Canal service, the *Chevalier*, used for much of her career on the Crinan to Corpach service, and the little *Linnet*, which introduced steam passenger services through the Crinan canal.

At this time the title 'The Royal Route' was first promoted, i.e. from Glasgow to Ardrishaig by *Iona*, later *Columba*, from Ardrishaig to Crinan by *Linnet*, from Crinan to Oban and Corpach by *Chevalier*, from Banavie at the top of the lock staircase to Inverness by *Gondolier*. This route was named because Queen Victoria had travelled it in 1847.

In 1878 *Columba*, the most famous Clyde steamer ever built, was launched, serving as the summer steamers on the Glasgow to Ardrishaig Royal Mail service until 1935. She was the longest passenger steamer ever built for the Firth of Clyde, and one of the first to have a steel hull. Her facilities included a hairdressing salon and a post office on board. Prior to 1914, the landed classes used her en route to their highland shooting lodges as well as day excursion passengers from the Greater Glasgow and Clyde Coast area.

In 1876 David Hutcheson retired, in 1878 Alexander Hutcheson retired, and from the following year David MacBrayne operated on the business in his own name. A succession of steamers appeared over the next quarter of a century, some passenger and some cargo, some paddle and some screw, some new and some second hand, some to have long lives in the West Highlands, others to be wrecked or sold after only a short period in service. Notable amongst these were the screw *Claymore* of 1881, and the paddlers *Grenadier* (1885), which made her name on the round Mull trip to Staffa and Iona from Oban, and *Fusilier* (1888).

The latter part of the nineteenth century saw the arrival of the railway at west-coast ports. The Dingwall & Skye Railway, part of the Highland Railway from 1880, was opened to Strome Ferry in 1870, and on the Kyle of Lochalsh in 1897. The Callander & Oban Railway later part of the Caledonian Railway reached Oban in 1880. The West Highland Railway, part of the North British Railway, reached Fort William in 1894, and the West Highland Extension reached Mallaig in 1901. David MacBrayne co-operated with the railway companies and the pattern of long-distance services from Glasgow was replaced by shorter services from the railheads, particularly Oban, which became known as 'The Charing Cross of the Highlands'. In 1880 the Highland Railway Company had ceased their shipping operations from Strome Ferry, and MacBrayne obtained the Royal Mail contract from Strome Ferry, later Kyle of Lochalsh, to Portree and Stornoway. In the late 1880s MacBrayne operated a short-lived service to Iceland.

In 1902 David MacBrayne retired, leaving his son David Hope MacBrayne to run the company. In 1906 the business was converted to a private limited company, David MacBrayne Ltd, and in 1907 David MacBrayne died. In that year, the first motor vessels arrived in the fleet, the *Comet* and the *Scout*, also the magnificent screw steamer *Chieftain*, one of the largest steamers to be owned by MacBraynes. The following year the larger motor vessel *Lochinvar* appeared for the Sound of Mull service. Initially all these three motor vessels had paraffin engines. In the early years of the last century an aluminium smelter was built at Kinlochleven and a new service was operated to there from Ballachulish.

MacBraynes survived the First World War with only two vessels, the second *Lochiel* and the little cargo steamer *Dirk*, being lost, and with only one paddle steamer, the *Grenadier*, being requisitioned as a minesweeper.

By the late twenties, the fleet was ageing, and 1927 was truly an 'annus horribilis' for the company. On New Years day, the *Sheila*, en route to Stornoway, was lost after running aground off the mouth of Loch Torridon. On 27 March, the *Chevalier* ran aground on Barmore Island, north or Tarbert on Loch Fyne, whilst on the winter Ardrishaig mail service, and on 5 September *Grenadier* was lost by fire whilst berthed at Oban overnight.

In 1928, with MacBraynes on the verge of bankruptcy, the company's tender for the mail contract was withdrawn and a joint application was made to purchase the company and operate the mail runs by Sir Alfred Read, Chairman and managing Director of the Coast Lines group, and Sir Josiah Stamp, President of the London Midland & Scottish Railway Company. A new jointly owned company, David MacBrayne (1928) Limited, was formed. Part of the deal was that four new ships were to be introduced over the next two years.

These duly appeared, the steamer *Lochness* in 1929, motor vessels *Lochearn* and *Lochmor* in 1930 and the diesel-electric *Lochfyne* in 1931. In 1934 a further motorship, *Lochnevis*, was built and the business of Alexander Paterson, who had operated the small steamer *Princess Louise* on local excursions at Oban, was taken over. The old steamers were going in this period as well, *Glencoe* in 1931 and *Iona* and *Columba* after the 1935 season.

In October 1935, the fleets of Williamson-Buchanan steamers and Turbine Steamers Ltd were taken over by the LMSR and two of the latter company's fleet were allocated to MacBraynes. These were *Queen Alexandra* of 1912 which gained a third funnel and ran as *Saint Columba* on the summer Ardrishaig Mail service until 1958, and *King George V*, which was the indirect replacement for the *Grenadier* on the Staffa and Iona trip, which she maintained until 1974. Some other additions to the fleet at this period were transfers from other companies in the Coast Lines group.

1939 saw a new motorship for the Islay mail service, *Lochiel*, replacing the last paddle steamer in the fleet, *Pioneer*. The Second World War saw twenty vessels being taken up for government service, some being purchased and not returned after the war, but only one, *Lochgarry*, being lost, and that by running around in a storm and not be enemy action.

In November 1947, the firm of McCallum, Orme & Co. Ltd were taken over with their venerable steamers *Dunara Castle* and *Hebrides*, which operated from Glasgow to various ports in the Western Isles, and had served St Kilda prior to the evacuation of the inhabitants of that island in 1930.

On 1 January 1948 the railways were nationalised and the 50% share of the LMSR was taken over by British Railways.

The post-war years saw a new motorship for the Stornoway mail service, *Loch Seaforth*, and series of new motor vessels for the cargo services from Glasgow. In 1955, the *Claymore* was introduced on the Barra and Lochboisdale mail service from Oban.

The need for car-ferry services to the Isles was finally met in 1964, when three lift-loading car ferries, *Columba*, *Hebrides* and *Clansman* appeared. Previously cars had been crane-loaded on the mail vessels. These served Craignure, Mull, from Oban, Tarbert, Harris and Lochmaddy, North Uist from Uig, and Armadale from Mallaig respectively.

In 1969 the Government set up the Scottish Transport Group, to operate the nationalised bus services in Scotland and the fleets of the Caledonian Steam Packet Ltd on the Clyde and David MacBrayne in the West Highlands. On 1 July of that year they purchased Coast Lines' 50% share in MacBraynes.

One of the Clyde car ferries, *Arran*, was transferred to the Islay service, and a car ferry, which had been building for that service, the *Iona*, commenced operations on the Clyde.

On 1 January 1973, the CSP and MacBraynes were merged as Caledonian MacBrayne Ltd, although the cargo vessels and some of the smaller passenger ferries remained under the ownership of David MacBrayne Ltd for a further spell until the last cargo service was withdrawn in 1976.

STEAM COMMUNICATION

BETWEEN

GLASGOW AND THE HIGHLANDS.

THE NEW STEAMERS,

CYGNET, LAPWING, AND DUNTROON CASTLE,

ARE INTENDED TO SAIL, AS UNDERNOTED, FOR

OBAN, TOBERMORY, PORTREE,

FORT-WILLIAM, INVERNESS,

AND INTERMEDIATE PORTS,

Unless prevented by any unforeseen occurrence, till further notice.

Glasgow, Oban, Fort-William, and Inverness.

FROM GLASGOW.

Thursday,	-	-	6th February,	-	-	at 6 Morning.
Monday,	-	-	10th ″	-	-	at 11 Forenoon.
Thursday,	-	-	13th ″	-	-	at 6 Morning.
Thursday,	-	-	20th ″	-	-	at 6 Morning.
Monday,	-	-	24th ″	-	-	at 11 Forenoon.
Thursday,	-	-	27th ″	-	-	at 6 Morning.

FROM INVERNESS.

Monday,	-	-	3d February,	-	-	at 6 Morning.
Monday,	-	-	10th ″	-	-	at 6 Morning.
Thursday,	-	-	13th ″	-	-	at 6 Morning.
Monday,	-	-	17th ″	-	-	at 6 Morning.
Monday,	-	-	24th ″	-	-	at 6 Morning.
Thursday,	-	-	27th ″	-	-	at 6 Morning.

Glasgow, Oban, and Tobermory.

FROM GLASGOW.

Monday,	-	-	3d February,	-	-	at 11 Forenoon.
Thursday,	-	-	13th ″	-	-	at 2 Afternoon
Monday,	-	-	17th ″	-	-	at 11 Forenoon.
Thursday,	-	-	27th ″	-	-	at 2 Afternoon

FROM TOBERMORY.

Wednesday,	-	-	5th February,	-	-	-	Morning.
Tuesday,	-	-	18th ″	-	-	-	Morning.
Wednesday,	-	-	19th ″	-	-	-	Morning.
Tuesday,	-	-	4th March,	-	-	-	Morning.

Glasgow, Oban, Tobermory, and Portree.

FROM GLASGOW.

Thursday,	-	-	13th February,	-	-	at 2 Afternoon
Thursday,	-	-	27th ″	-	-	at 2 Afternoon

FROM PORTREE.

Tuesday,	-	-	18th February,	-	-	Morning.
Tuesday,	-	-	4th March,	-	-	Morning.

The "DUNTROON CASTLE" will call (weather permitting) at the intermediate Ports of CRAIGNURE, LOCHALINE, SALEN, ARISAIG, ARMADALE, ISLE ORNSAY, GLENELG, BALMACARRA, KYLEAKIN, and BROADFORD.

The Freight of all Goods must be paid at Shipment, except for those places at which there are regular Agents.

The Company not responsible for Dogs; nor for Luggage, unless paid and signed for by them or their Agents; nor for any damage Goods may sustain in landing or shipping at any of the Ferries; nor for any Goods until they are actually received on board.—The only places where they have recognised Agents are those noted below.

ALEX. M'CULLOCH, Greenock.	ALEX. M'DONALD, Portree.
DUNCAN M'ARTHUR, Oban.	ALEX. BROWN, Fort-William.
JAMES GRAHAM, Tobermory.	MASSON & PATERSON, Inverness.

Or here to

GEORGE & JAMES BURNS,

9, Buchanan Street, Glasgow.

Glasgow, Feb. 1, 1851.

Hutcheson, Alexander Hutcheson & Co

1851.

STEAM COMMUNICATION

BETWEEN

GLASGOW AND THE HIGHLANDS.

THE New Steamers CYGNET, LAPWING, and DUNTROON CASTLE, are intended to Sail, as under-noted, for OBAN, TOBERMORY, PORTREE, FORT-WILLIAM, INVERNESS, and Intermediate Ports, unless prevented by any unforeseen occurrence, till further Notice

GLASGOW, OBAN, FORT-WILLIAM, & INVERNESS.

FROM GLASGOW.	FROM INVERNESS.
Thursday, Feb. 13, at 6 a.m.	Thursday, Feb. 13, at 6 a.m.
Thursday, — 20, at 6 a.m.	Monday, — 17, at 6 a.m.
Monday, — 24, at 11 a.m.	Monday, — 24, at 6 a.m.
Thursday, — 27, at 6 a.m.	Thursday, — 27, at 6 a.m.

GLASGOW, OBAN, & TOBERMORY.

FROM GLASGOW.	FROM TOBERMORY.
Thursday, Feb. 13, at 2 p.m.	Tuesday, — 18, Morning.
Monday, — 17, at 11 a.m.	Wednesday, — 19, Morning.
Thursday, — 27, at 2 p.m.	Tuesday, March 4, Morning.

GLASGOW, OBAN, TOBERMORY, & PORTREE.

FROM GLASGOW.	FROM PORTREE.
Thursday, Feb. 13, at 2 p.m.	Tuesday, Feb. 18, Morning.
Thursday, — 27, at 2 p.m.	Tuesday, March 4, Morning.

The "DUNTROON CASTLE" will call (weather permitting) at the Intermediate Ports of CRAIGNURE, LOCHALINE, SALEN, ARISAIG, ARMADALE, ISLE ORNSAY, GLENELG, BALMACARRA, KYLEAKIN, and BROADFORD.

Apply to Wm. Lindsay & Co., Greenock; Duncan M'Arthur, Oban; James Graham, Tobermory; Alex. M'Donald, Portree; Alex. Brown, Fort-William; Masson & Paterson, Inverness; or, here to

DAVID HUTCHESON & CO.,

14 Jamaica Street, Glasgow.

Glasgow, 10th February, 1851.

The transition to Hutchesons. To the left an advert for George & James Burns for the *Cygnet*, *Lapwing* and *Duntroon Castle* dated 1 Feb 1851. To the right an advert for the same steamers and same destinations dated 10 February 1851 placed by David Hutcheson & Co. *Cygnet* and *Lapwing* were sisters dating from 1848 and lasting until lost in 1882 and 1858 respectively, while *Duntroon Castle* had been built in 1842 and was sold in 1853. (GEL).

One
Hutcheson's Steamers
1851-1879

David Hutcheson is commemorated by this monument, errected in 1883, on the north end of Kerrera, easily visible from Oban, and photographed here with P S *Waverley* in the foreground on 7 May 2001, as near to the 150th anniversary of Hutcheson as was possible with a paddle steamer. The inscription reads:

> *'Erected by a grateful public in memory of David Hutcheson, by whose energy and enterprise the benefits of greatly improved steam communication were conferred on the West Highlands and Islands of Scotland'.*

Loch Ness and Foyers Pier

Glengarry had been built in 1844 by Smith and Rodger as *Edinburgh Castle* for the Glasgow to Holy Loch service. In 1846 she was transferred to the Caledonian Canal and was part of the Thomson & McConnell fleet, coming under the ownership of Hutchesons in 1851. In 1875 she was altered and short deck saloons added. She is seen at Foyers pier whilst on the Loch Ness mail service, which she served until December 1927, following which she was broken up at Inverness.

Pioneer was built in 1844 by Barr and McNab of Paisley for the Glasgow, Paisley, &Greenock Railway Company's service from Glasgow to Greenock and Rothesay. In February 1847 she was taken over by G.&J. Burns, who in 1851 transferred her to Hutcheson when the latter took over their West Highland services. She was on the Glasgow to Ardrishaig service in that year. On being replaced by *Mountaineer* the following year, she moved to Oban, where she operated three days a week to Staffa and Iona, and three days a week to Corpach and Fort William, a roster not too dissimilar with that operated by *King George V* some 120 years later. In 1874-1875 she was lengthened and deck saloons and a second funnel added. She continued in service until 1893, finally being scrapped in August 1895. Pioneer is shown here at Oban in her condition prior to 1874.

Mountaineer was the first steamer to be built for Messrs Hutcheson, and was his favourite ship, being built by J.&G. Thomson at Govan in 1852, and initially used on the Ardrishaig service. In 1855 she was replaced by the first *Iona* and was transferred to Oban for the Staffa and Iona and Fort William services, also appearing at times of the Crinan route. In 1876 she was fitted with deck saloons.

On 27 September 1889 *Mountaineer* ran aground on the Lady Rock, near Lismore, and was unable to be salvaged. (GEL)

Mary Jane was built in 1846 by Tod & McGregor for James (later Sir James) Matheson of Stornoway and named after his wife. She sailed on the Glasgow to Stornoway route and was sold in 1851 to the Glasgow and Lochfine Steam Packet Company for the Glasgow to Inveraray run. In 1857 that company was taken over by Hutcheson, and *Mary Jane* continued on the Loch Fyne service until 1875. She is seen here at Tarbert, Loch Fyne in 1858. (A Fraser Collection).

In 1875, *Mary Jane* was renamed *Glencoe*, her bowsprit was removed and a deck saloon fitted aft. Initially she operated on a variety of routes, but from 1890 to 1905 she was on the West Loch Tarbert to Islay mail run, and is seen here at the original pier at West Loch Tarbert.

From 1905 until May 1931, when she was withdrawn, *Glencoe* operated the service from Mallaig and Kyle of Lochalsh to Portree with few exceptions. She is seen here off Kyle of Lochalsh. (QRC).

GLENCOE, LOCHEARN & LOCHMOR.

In March 1931 both *Lochearn* and *Lochmor* broke down off Kyleakin and *Glencoe* had to be called in to tow them into Kyle of Lochalsh Railway Pier. (RB)

Following her withdrawal from service, *Glencoe* was exhibited at Glasgow on 4 June 1931 along with the new *Lochfyne* as part of Glasgow Civic Week. *Glencoe* was scrapped at Ardrossan in autumn 1931 at the venerable age of eighty-five. (CRSC).

Inveraray Castle was also acquired by Hutchesons with the Glasgow & Lochfine Steam Packet Company. She had been built in 1839 by Tod and McGregor and operated on the Glasgow to Inveraray cargo service for almost all her career until broken up at Bowling in 1892.

Hutchesons' first screw steamer was *Fingal*, built in 1861 by J.&G. Thomson for the Stornoway service. After only four months service she was sold for blockade-running in the American Civil War. She made only one run, inwards to Savannah with a cargo including 11,000 rifles, 2 cannons, and 24,000 pounds of gunpowder, arriving there on 14 November 1861. Trapped there, she was taken over by the Confederate Navy, converted to an ironclad, and renamed CSS *Atlanta*. In June 1863 she was captured by Union forces and commissioned into the Union Navy the following February as USS *Atlanta*, in which guise she is seen here, in the James River, Virginia. She was sold in May 1869 and reportedly became the Haitian warship *Triumph* being lost at sea off Cape Hatteras in December 1869. (USNHS).

Clydesdale was built by J.&G. Thomson in 1862 to take the place of the *Fingal* on the Glasgow to Stornoway service. In 1893 she was re-boilered and a second funnel was added, as seen here. From 1889 she was placed on a service from Oban to the outer Islands, with occasional calls at St. Kilda. In January 1905, she ran aground on the Lady Rock and was later dismantled.

Staffa came in 1863 from J.&G. Thomson, who were by now getting established as the regular shipbuilders for David Hutcheson and Co. She operated mainly on the Glasgow to Inverness service via the Mull of Kintyre, and ran aground on Cathsgeir Rock off the west of Gigha in August 1886. All passengers were safely landed and the next day she broke in two and sank.

A drawing of the second *Iona* from the *Illustrated London News*. She appeared in 1863 on the Glasgow to Ardrishaig service. Her predecessor of the same name had been built in 1855 and was similar, but flush-decked. She replaced the *Mountaineer* on the Ardrishaig service and was sold in autumn 1862 for blockade running in the US Civil War, but was run down off Gourock by the steamer *Chanticleer* and sank. The second *Iona* was also sold for blockade running after only one season in service. Her deck salons were removed, and used on her successor, but she was little luckier than her predecessor, and was sunk off Lundy Island on 2 February 1864. (GEL)

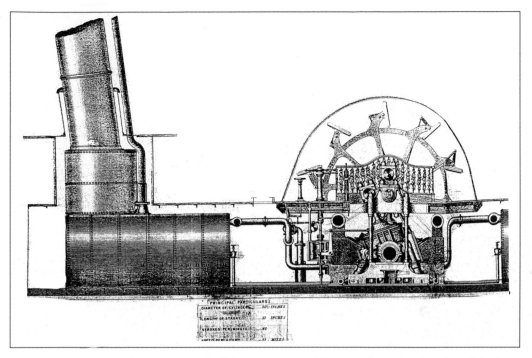

A cross-section from the same source of the engines, paddles, one funnel and boiler of the *Iona* of 1863. She was powered, like her predecessor and successor, and further paddle steamers up to the *Grenadier*, by two-cylinder, simple expansion, oscillating engines. (GEL).

Iona was built in 1864 to replace her predecessor of the same name on the Glasgow to Ardrishaig service, and was fitted with the deck saloons of the earlier vessel. In 1873 she was fitted with steam steering gear, being one of the first ships to be fitted with this. Replaced on the main Ardrishaig service by *Columba* in 1878, she was used for a number of years on a secondary Ardrishaig service, offering a 10.40 departure from Wemyss Bay from 1904 onwards. She is seen here arriving at Dunoon.

After the First World War, *Iona* operated in a Lochgoilhead and Arrochar service until 1927, and she is seen here on that service, at Douglas Pier on Loch Goil. (GEL)

Following the loss of the *Chevalier*, *Iona* was placed on the Oban to Fort William route from 1927 until withdrawal after the 1935 season. She is seen here approaching Kentallen. (CRSC)

Iona at Kentallen pier in 1935. The buildings in this view are still in existence today, the larger one (the former railway station) is now a hotel.

Gondolier was the first of three steamers to join the fleet in 1866. She spent her entire career of seventy-three years on the Caledonian Canal route from Inverness to Banavie. She is seen here at Banavie, with the connecting train from Fort William to the left, the branch railway having opened in 1895.

Kyltra Lock.   Caledonian Canal.

Archd. Macintyre, Fort William

Gondolier in Kyltra Lock, between Loch Oich and Fort Augustus.

Looking up the Lochs, Caledonian Canal.   Fort Augustus.

Archd Macintyre, Fort William

Gondolier descending the flight of Locks leading down to Loch Ness at Fort Augustus.

A stern view of *Gondolier* in the locks at Fort Augustus.

Gondolier at journey's end, Inverness. This view shows her fore saloon after it had been rebuilt in 1935. The steamer was withdrawn after the 1939 summer season, and acquired by the Admiralty in 1940. Her machinery, paddle boxes and saloons were removed and she was taken to Scapa Flow where she was sunk as a blockship.

The second steamer to be built in 1866 was the *Chevalier*. From 1886 until 1914 she was used on the Crinan-Oban-Fort-William-Corpach service. She is seen here off Crinan.

Chevalier at Crinan. Passengers travelling north on the Royal Route would join her here from the *Linnet*, which had carried them through the Crinan Canal from Ardrishaig.

On 25 March, 1927, whilst on the winter Ardrishaig service, *Chevalier* met her end. En route from Tarbert to Ardrishaig, her starboard paddle wheel fractured during a gale, and she drifted onto rocks at Barmore Island, north of Tarbert. The passengers were brought safely ashore, and the steamer freed herself after several days.

She was towed to Troon for breaking up, as seen here. (QRC).

S.S. "Linnet" passing Bellanoch

Neil Smith, Cairnbaan Store, Crinan Canal

The third steamer of 1866 was the little *Linnet*, which replaced the horse-drawn track boats *Sunbeam* and *Maid of Perth* on the Crinan Canal service, connecting the *Iona*, and later *Columba*, at Ardrishaig, with the *Chevalier* at Crinan. She is seen here passing Bellanoch with a large passenger load.

S.S. "LINNET" AT CAIRNBAAN STORE

Linnet, known as 'the floating tram', passing Cairnbaan near the mid-point of the Canal.

Another postcard view of *Linnet* at Cairnbaan, this time from above lock 6.

A stern view of *Linnet*, showing the raised steering platform, which was fitted in 1894.

Linnet at Crinan, with a steam drifter having come up through the locks from the sea.

Linnet was withdrawn in September 1929, the leg of the Royal Route from Ardrishaig to Oban thenceforth being provided by bus. She was sold to the Glasgow Motor Boat Racing Club and moored in the Gareloch at Shandon as a clubhouse, fitted with a deckhouse, which had come off the *Lord of the Isles*, until wrecked in a storm in January 1932. She is seen here with two unidentified laid up cargo steamers in the background. (GEL).

Dolphin had been built as the *Islay* in 1849 by Tod & McGregor for the West Loch Tarbert to Islay service, although she later operated from Glasgow to Oban and Portree. She was purchased by Hutchesons in February 1868, and renamed *Dolphin*. In June 1868 she was sailing on charter on the Glasgow to Stranraer route, and in July she was sold to the Donaghadee & Port Patrick Short Sea Steam Packet Company, sailing between these two ports for the remainder of that summer. She was sold on to London owners the following year.

Clansman was built in 1870 for the Glasgow to Stornoway route, which she served until laid up at Bowling in 1909, being scrapped the following year. (QRC).

First-Class RETURN TICKETS to INVERNESS, &c., available during the Season.
. By Act of Parliament, a Transit Duty is leviable on all Passengers passing through the Crinan and Caledonian Canals. Transit Duty Tickets Issued on Board the Steamers.

SWIFTEST STEAM CONVEYANCE
By the ROYAL ROUTE (via Crinan and Caledonian Canals) between
GLASGOW & THE HIGHLANDS.

WITH PASSENGERS ONLY.   *The Royal Mail Steamers*   WITH GOODS AND PASSENGERS.

IONA,	CHEVALIER,	CLANSMAN,	CLYDESDALE,
GONDOLIER,	LINNET,	CYGNET,	PLOVER,
MOUNTAINEER,	PIONEER,	STAFFA,	MARY JANE,
AND EDINBURGH CASTLE.		AND INVERARAY CASTLE.	

UNLESS PREVENTED BY WEATHER OR ANY UNFORESEEN OCCURRENCE, UNTIL FURTHER NOTICE,
THE ROYAL MAIL STEAMER "IONA," or other Steamer, will leave GLASGOW BRIDGE WHARF every Morning (Sunday excepted) at 7 o'Clock, direct for GREENOCK, from thence about 9 A.M., on arrival of the 7·40 A.M. Train, for
KIRN, DUNOON, INNELLAN, ROTHESAY, KYLES OF BUTE, TARBERT, & ARDRISHAIG,
Leaving ARDRISHAIG for GLASGOW, DAILY, about 12·45 P.M., and calling at the above-named places in returning.
Passengers for OBAN and the NORTH Change at Ardrishaig, and are conveyed along the Crinan Canal by Steamer "LINNET" to Crinan, and thence by "CHEVALIER," or other Steamer, to Oban, &c.

GOING NORTH.

GLASGOW TO INVERNESS,
By CRINAN, LUING, EASDALE, OBAN, APPIN, BALLACHULISH PIER, ARDGOUR PIER (CORRAN), FORT-WILLIAM, CORPACH, BANAVIE, and CALEDONIAN CANAL. CALLING AT THE FALLS OF FOYERS.
By the IONA, or other Steamer, DAILY (except Sunday)............at 7 A.M.
Train to Greenock at 7·40 A.M.—arriving at Oban in the afternoon about 4·45, Fort-William 7·30 P.M., Corpach and Banavie about 8 same evening, and Inverness on afternoon of following day. Passengers on Saturday remain at Banavie until Monday morning.
Cabin Passengers only are conveyed by Omnibus from Corpach to Banavie.

GLASGOW TO FORT-WILLIAM, CORPACH, & BANAVIE.
By the IONA, or other Steamer, DAILY (except Sunday)............at 7 A.M.
Train to Greenock at 7·40 A.M.; arriving at Oban about 4·45 P.M., Fort-William, 7·30 P.M., Corpach and Banavie about 8 the same evening.

GLASGOW TO OBAN.
By the IONA, or other Steamer, DAILY (except Sunday)............at 7 A.M.
Train to Greenock at 7·40 A.M.; arriving at Oban same afternoon about 4·45.

GLASGOW TO SOUND OF MULL & TOBERMORY.
Train to Greenock at 7·40 A.M., arriving same afternoon. Passengers change Steamer at Oban.............at 7 A.M.

OBAN TO FORT-WILLIAM, CORPACH, & BANAVIE.
By Steamer CHEVALIER, every AFTERNOON (except Sunday),......about 4·45 o'clock.
By Steamer MOUNTAINEER or PIONEER, every MONDAY, TUESDAY, WEDNESDAY, THURSDAY, and FRIDAY, at 7 A.M.

BANAVIE TO INVERNESS.
By Steamer GONDOLIER or EDINBURGH, DAILY (except Sunday)............at 8 A.M.
CALLING AT THE FALLS OF FOYERS.

OBAN TO SOUND OF MULL, SKYE, & GAIRLOCH.
By the Swift Steamer PIONEER, from OBAN, every FRIDAY, at 7·30 A.M., calling at Craignure, Lochaline, Salen, Aros Pier, Tobermory, Armadale, Glenelg, Balmacarra, Kyleakin, Broadford, and Portree. The Steamer will call at Loch-Hourn on the trip to Portree, and Loch-Duich on the return voyage, weather and other circumstances permitting; and will proceed from Portree every SATURDAY, at 6 A.M., for Gairloch, and return again same evening to Portree.

GLASGOW TO TOBERMORY, PORTREE, & STORNOWAY,
By OBAN.
The CLANSMAN, or other Steamer, via Mull of Kintyre, every THURSDAY, from Glasgow, at 12 Noon; Train to Greenock at 4·45 P.M. Calling at CRAIGNURE, LOCHALINE, SALEN, AROS PIER, ARMADALE, GLENELG, BALMACARRA, KYLEAKIN, BROADFORD, and any other place that may be agreed upon. Passengers by the Swift Steamer on Thursday to Oban may join the CLANSMAN there on Friday Morning.
The CLYDESDALE, or other Steamer, via Mull of Kintyre, every MONDAY, at 8 A.M.; Train to Greenock at 11 A.M. Calling at CRAIGNURE, LOCHALINE, SALEN, AROS PIER, ARISAIG, ARMADALE, ISLE ORNSAY, GLENELG, BALMACARRA, KYLEAKIN, BROADFORD, and any other place that may be agreed upon. Passengers by Swift Steamer on Monday may join the CLYDESDALE on Tuesday Morning at Oban.

GLASGOW TO ULLAPOOL & LOCHINVER.
The CLYDESDALE, on MONDAYS, 8th & 22nd July, 5th & 19th August............at 8 A.M.
Train at 11 A.M.
It is in the option of the Captain to call at either place first.

GLASGOW TO GAIRLOCH & AULTBEA.
The CLANSMAN, on THURSDAYS, 4th & 18th July, 1st, 15th & 29th August.....at 12 Noon.
Train at 4·45 P.M. Calling on the Voyage to Stornoway.

GLASGOW TO LOCHMADDY & TARBERT (HARRIS).
The CLYDESDALE, on MONDAYS, 1st, 15th, & 29th July, 12th & 26th August............at 8 A.M.
Train at 11 A.M. Calling on the Voyage to Stornoway.

COMING SOUTH.

INVERNESS TO GLASGOW.
By CALEDONIAN CANAL, BANAVIE, CORPACH, FORT-WILLIAM, ARDGOUR PIER (CORRAN), BALLACHULISH PIER, APPIN, OBAN, EASDALE, LUING, CRAIGNISH, CRINAN, ARDRISHAIG, TARBERT, KYLES OF BUTE, ROTHESAY, INNELLAN, DUNOON, KIRN, and GREENOCK. CALLING AT THE FALLS OF FOYERS.
By Steamer GONDOLIER or EDINBURGH, every MONDAY, TUESDAY, WEDNESDAY, THURSDAY, and FRIDAY, at 7 A.M., arriving at Oban the same afternoon, and Glasgow the following day; and every SATURDAY, at 10·30 A.M., remaining at Banavie until Monday morning.
Passengers only are conveyed from Banavie to Corpach.

CORPACH & FORT-WILLIAM TO GLASGOW.
By CHEVALIER, or other Steamer.....................DAILY (except Sunday), leaving Corpach about 5·15 A.M., and Fort-William, about 5·30 A.M., arriving at Glasgow same afternoon.

OBAN TO GLASGOW,
By EASDALE, LUING, CRAIGNISH, CRINAN, ARDRISHAIG, TARBERT, KYLES OF BUTE, ROTHESAY, INNELLAN, DUNOON, KIRN, and GREENOCK.
By CHEVALIER or other Steamer, DAILY (except Sunday), at 8 A.M., arriving at Glasgow same afternoon.

TOBERMORY & SOUND OF MULL TO GLASGOW.
Every THURSDAY Morning.................at 5·30 A.M. per Swift Steamer via Crinan Canal, arriving at Glasgow same afternoon. Passengers change Steamer at Oban.

CORPACH & FORT-WILLIAM TO OBAN.
By Steamer CHEVALIER, DAILY (except Sunday), leaving Corpach about 5·15 A.M. and Fort-William about 5·30 A.M.; and by Steamer MOUNTAINEER or PIONEER, every MONDAY, TUESDAY, WEDNESDAY, THURSDAY, and FRIDAY Afternoon, on arrival of Steamer from Inverness.

INVERNESS TO BANAVIE,
By Steamer GONDOLIER of EDINBURGH, every MONDAY, TUESDAY, WEDNESDAY, THURSDAY, and FRIDAY, at 7 A.M.; and every SATURDAY, at 10·30 A.M., except on 13th July, when the Steamer will leave at 2 P.M.
CALLING AT THE FALLS OF FOYERS.

INVERNESS TO OBAN.
By CALEDONIAN CANAL. The Steamer GONDOLIER of EDINBURGH, every MONDAY, TUESDAY, WEDNESDAY, THURSDAY, and FRIDAY, at 7 A.M., arriving at Oban same afternoon.

GAIRLOCH, PORTREE, SOUND OF SKYE, & MULL TO OBAN.
By the Swift Steamer PIONEER, every MONDAY, at 5 A.M., from Portree for Oban and intermediate places. The Steamer will leave Portree for Gairloch every SATURDAY Morning, and return again to Portree same evening.

STORNOWAY, PORTREE, & TOBERMORY TO GLASGOW,
By OBAN, with Goods and Passengers.
The CLANSMAN, or other Steamer, from STORNOWAY, every MONDAY, and from Portree, on TUESDAYS, not earlier than 4 A.M. Calling at BROADFORD, KYLEAKIN, BALMACARRA, GLENELG, ARMADALE, AROS PIER, SALEN, LOCHALINE, and CRAIGNURE, arriving at Oban on Tuesday, and Glasgow on Wednesday.
The CLYDESDALE, or other Steamer, every WEDNESDAY from STORNOWAY, and every THURSDAY (except) on 18th July, when the Steamer will sail on the 19th) from PORTREE, not earlier than 6 A.M. Calling at BROADFORD, KYLEAKIN, BALMACARRA, GLENELG, ISLE ORNSAY, ARMADALE, ARISAIG, AROS PIER, SALEN, LOCHALINE, and CRAIGNURE, arriving at Oban same afternoon, and Glasgow on Friday.

GLASGOW & ISLAY.
By the IONA, or other Steamer, every TUESDAY, at 7 A.M., Train to Greenock at 7·40 A.M. to EAST TARBERT, thence per Steamer ISLAY from WEST TARBERT to ISLAY.
Leaving ISLAY every TUESDAY Morning for GLASGOW, via TARBERT.

GLASGOW TO INVERARAY.
By the IONA, or other Steamer, to Ardrishaig, from thence by MARY JANE of INVERARAY CASTLE to Inveraray. See Sailings of Cargo Steamers.

GLASGOW TO SCRABSTER ROADS, THURSO.
On 11th and 15th July.

From OBAN for STAFFA and IONA,
By Swift Steamer MOUNTAINEER or PIONEER, every TUESDAY, THURSDAY, and SATURDAY, returning same evening.

From OBAN for (BALLACHULISH) GLENCOE,
By Swift Steamer MOUNTAINEER or PIONEER, every MONDAY, TUESDAY, WEDNESDAY, THURSDAY, and FRIDAY, returning same evening.

From OBAN for SOUND OF MULL, SKYE, & GAIRLOCH, Ross-shire.
The Swift Steamer PIONEER is intended to leave Oban, until further notice, every FRIDAY, at 7·30 A.M., for the SOUND OF MULL, SKYE, PORTREE, &c., leaving Portree for Gairloch every SATURDAY Morning at 6 o'clock, returning again from Portree same afternoon. Tourists will thus have an opportunity of viewing the Magnificent Scenery of SKYE, LOCH-HOURN, LOCH-DUICH, and LOCH-MAREE. FARES, from Oban to Gairloch—Cabin, 30s. RETURN TICKETS—Cabin, 37s. 6d.
These Vessels afford in their passages a View of the Beautiful Scenery of the Clyde, all its Watering-Places—the Island and Kyles of Bute—Sound of Kyles—Mountains of Arran—Mountains of Cowal, Knapdale, and Kintyre—Lochfyne—Crinan—with the Islands of Jura, Scarba, Mull, and many others of the Western Sea—the Whirlpool of Corryvreckan—the Mountains of Lorn, of Morven, of Appin of Kingairloch, and Ben-Nevis—Inverlochy—the Lands of Lochiel, the scene of the Wanderings of Prince Charles, and near to where the Clans raised his Standard in the '45—Lochaber—the Caledonian Canal—Loch Lochy—Loch Oich—Loch Ness, with the Glens and Mountains on either side, and the celebrated FALLS OF FOYERS. Books descriptive of the route may be had on board the Steamers.

Carriages and Horses taken by the Swift Boats, provided there are Persons in charge.
Passengers allowed Half a Cwt. of Luggage free, all beyond that quantity to be charged at the rate of 8s. per Cwt. Passengers going by the "IONA," or other Steamer, are requested to send as much of their Luggage as they can to the Luggage Boats, as it will save them time, trouble, and expense in transhipping. The Company not responsible for Dogs; nor for Luggage, unless paid and signed for by them or their Agents. For further particulars apply to the following Agents—

Wm. Lindsay & Co., GREENOCK.	Turner & Mackintosh, INVERNESS.	Daniel M'Alister, STORNOWAY.
Alex. Brown, OBAN.	John Masson, TOBERMORY.	Thomas M'Kenzie, Innkeeper, PORTREE.
John Murdoch, FORT-WILLIAM.	John Campbell, PORTREE.	Kenneth Cameron, ULLAPOOL.

GLASGOW, 1st July, 1867.   OR HERE, TO THE PROPRIETORS,   DAVID HUTCHESON & CO., 119 Hope Street, Corner of Bothwell St.

A David Hutcheson and Co. timetable poster for July 1867.

The "Clansman" at Stornoway

Clansman at Stornoway, on a postcard posted in 1909 with the funnel of one of Langland's steamers behind her to the right.

Islay was built in 1867 by Barclay Curle to succeed her predecessor of the same name, which became Hutcheson's *Dolphin*, and was owned by C. Morrison, T.G. Buchanan and John Ramsey, serving the route from Glasgow to Portrush and Islay. In 1875 she was taken over by Hutchesons, serving on the same route without the call at Portrush. In 1882 she operated the Glasgow to Gairloch service. She was wrecked at Red Bay, Co. Antrim in December 1890. This is taken from a negative of a painting of her in the Langmuir collection. (GEL).

The first *Lochiel* was built by A.&J. Inglis in 1877 and served as a passenger and cargo steamer on various routes. She is seen here at West Loch Tarbert, where she operated the Islay service from 1879 to 1881. In 1907 she was ashore at Portree and was later broken up. She had a slightly smaller sister, named *Fingal*, also built in 1877, which was sold in 1917 to Liverpool owners, and sank in September of the same year.

Columba, built in 1878 by J.&G. Thomson, who had moved from Govan to Clydebank in 1872, was the final steamer to be built for David Hutcheson & Co. but spent the remainder of her long career after her first year, under MacBrayne ownership. She was the most notable steamer of the MacBrayne fleet. She operated the Glasgow to Ardrishaig summer service, with the exception of 1915, until her withdrawal in 1935. In her first season, 1878, there was no pier at Tarbert, and she landed passengers by ferry.

Columba was built to compete with the first *Lord of the Isles*, which ran to Inveraray. She is seen here racing the second *Lord of the Isles* in 1910 in Loch Fyne.

A stern view of *Columba*, taken in the evening of her career. She could be distinguished from *Iona* in that her saloons extended to the edge of the hull whereas those of *Iona* had alleyways running outside them. This view shows the upper deck and the two lifeboats, formerly on the *Scout*, which were added post Titanic, in 1914.

Columba arriving at Rothesay in a pre-1910 view with the NB's *Kenilworth* and the CSP's *Marchioness of Breadalbane* across the far end of the pier. From 1916 to 1918 she sailed from Wemyss Bay because of the boom between the Cloch and Dunoon.

Columba never sailed outside the Clyde. This is a faked postcard by Valentine's purportedly showing her from the inside of Fingal's Cave on Staffa.

SUMMER TOURS IN SCOTLAND BY DAVID MacBrayne's

Royal Mail Steamers

COLUMBA, IONA &c.

1/-

David MacBrayne published a hard-backed guidebook of Summer Tours to Scotland each year with timetables at the back of it. This is an illustration of *Columba* from the cover of the 1898 volume. These books are now highly collectable.

A deck view on *Columba* taken from a contemporary illustrated book.

In 1929 *Columba* was briefly painted, along with other members of the MacBrayne fleet, with a grey hull. This was repainted after a fortnight during the Glasgow Fair in the traditional black, because of a public outcry, and officially because a grey ship was difficult to make out at sea.

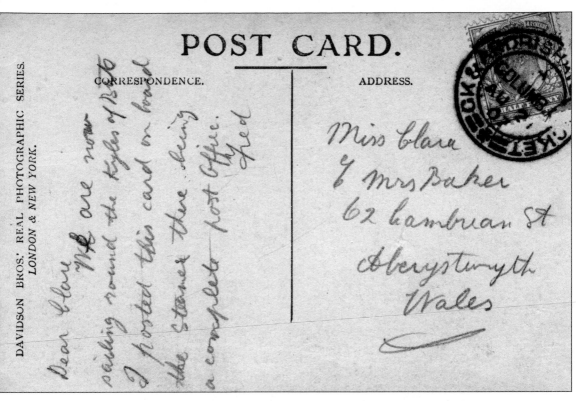

Columba had a post office on board, which had its own postmark. The message on this card reads, 'We are now sailing round the Kyles of Bute. I posted this card on board the steamer, there being a complete post office'. The Greenock & Ardrishaig Packet postmarks are much prized by philatelists, especially those featuring the names of winter relief steamers. The Post Office facility was withdrawn around 1914.

Columba in her final season, 1935, at her daily destination, Ardrishaig. Columba was withdrawn after the 1935 season and was sold, along with Iona, for scrapping at Arnott Youngs at Dalmuir.

TIME-TABLE for SEASON 1935

(June—September 30)

THROUGH SERVICE—Glasgow, Loch Fyne, Islay, Oban, Fort-William, Inverness and Intermediate Ports

The distance from the Stations to " Columba " Sailing Berth is comparatively short. See Street Plan on page 59.

GOING NORTH

R.M.S. " Columba "

	May 27 till Sept. 30 Daily Ex.Sun. a.m.
Glasgow (Bridge Wharf, South Side).........St'mr dep.	x7 11
Govan .... ,, ,,	x7 20
Glasgow (St. Enoch)..Train ,,	e7 30
Greenock (Princes Pier) St'mr ,,	9 0
Edinburgh (Prin. St.) Train ,,	c6 20
Glasgow (Central) .... ,, ,,	8 35
Gourock ....St'mr ,,	9 28
Edinburgh (Wav.)....Train ,,	6 25
Glasgow (Queen St.) ,, ,,	7 56
Dunoon ....St'mr ,,	9 45
Innellan .... ,, ,,	10 0
Rothesay .... ,, ,,	10 30
Colintraive .... ,, ,,	10 55
Tighnabruaich .... ,, ,,	11 10
‡Tarbert (for Islay—see below) ,, ,,	12 0n
Ardrishaig .... ,, arr.	12 45p

Motor Car — May 18 till Sept. 30 Daily

Ardrishaig..................dep.	1 10p
Oban ....arr.	3 20

Oban, Ballachulish (Kentallen Pier), and Fort-William — June 4 till Sept. 14 Tues., Thurs. and Sats.

Oban ....St'mr dep.	8 45a
Lismore .... ,, ,,	9 10
Kentallen (for Ballachulish),, ,,	10 0
Fort-William .... ,, arr.	10 55
Fort-William ....Train dep.	11 0
Banavie .... ,, arr.	11 9

Caledonian Canal

Banavie ....St'mr dep.	11 20a
Gairlochy .... ,, ,,	12 5p
Laggan .... ,, ,,	1 30
Cullochy .... ,, ,,	2 20
Fort-Augustus .... ,, ,,	3 40
Foyers .... ,, ,,	4 40
Temple Pier .... ,, ,,	5 10
Inverness............. ,, arr.	6 40

COMING SOUTH

Caledonian Canal — June 3 till Sept. 13 Mons., Weds., & Fris. a.m.

Inverness ....St'mr dep.	8 30
Foyers .... ,, ,,	10 25
Fort-Augustus .... ,, ,,	12 0n
Cullochy .... ,, ,,	12 50p
Laggan .... ,, ,,	1 45
Gairlochy .... ,, ,,	3 0
Banavie .... ,, arr.	3 50
Banavie ....Train dep.	4 14
Fort-William .... ,, arr.	4 23

Fort-William, Ballachulish (Kentallen Pier) and Oban

Fort-William ....St'mr dep.	4 30
Kentallen (for Ballachulish),, ,,	5 15
Lismore .... ,, ,,	6 15
Oban .... ,, arr.	6 40

Motor Car — May 18 till Sept. 30 Daily Ex.Sun. a.m.

Oban ....dep.	10 45
Ardrishaig.................arr.	12 45p

R.M.S. " Columba " — From May 27 till Sept. 30

Ardrishaig.............St'mr dep.	B1 10p
‡Tarbert .... ,, ,,	1 50
Tighnabruaich .... ,, ,,	2 50
Colintraive............ ,, ,,	3 5
Rothesay .... ,, ,,	3 40
Innellan .... ,, ,,	4 0
Dunoon .... ,, ,,	4 20
Glasgow (Queen St.)..Train arr.	D6 36
Edinburgh (Wav.).... ,, ,,	8 59
Gourock ....St'mr ,,	4 35
Glasgow (Central) ....Train ,,	d5 29
Edinburgh (Prin. St.) ,, ,,	8 6
Greenock (Princes Pier) St'mr ,,	4 55
Glasgow (St. Enoch)..Train ,,	G6 18
Govan ....St'mr ,,	x6 45
Glasgow (Bridge Wharf, South Side)........ ,, ,,	x6 55

Reference Notes.

c On Saturdays, 29th June to 31st August, inclusive, leaves at 7.6 a.m.

d Until 29th June, inclusive, arrives Glasgow (Central) 5.44 p.m.

e Leaves at 8.5 a.m. on Saturdays.

B From 16th Sept., departs at 1.0 p.m.

D On Saturdays arrives Glasgow (Queen St.) 6.20 p.m. Until 31st May, inclusive, arrives Glasgow (Queen St.) 7.42 p.m.

G Arrives at 6.22 p.m. on Saturdays.

x Sailings from and to Glasgow, 27th May to 14th Sept., thereafter from Greenock and Gourock only.

‡ Tarbert and Islay

	May 27 till Sept. 30		May 27 till Sept. 30
Tarbert E.....(Daily)..Coach dep.	12 0n	Port-Ellen ....St'mr dep.	8†30a
Tarbert W. ....St'mr ,,	12 50p	Gigha .... ,, ,,	10†10
Gigha .... ,, arr	2*30	Port-Askaig .... ,, ,,	8*30
Port-Ellen .... ,, ,,	4*45	Jura................... ,, ,,	9*30
Jura................. ,, ,,	3†30	Tarbert W. ...(Daily) ,, arr.	11 30
Port-Askaig .... ,, ,,	4†25	Tarbert E. ....Coach ,,	11 45

* Tuesdays, Thursdays and Saturdays.

† Mondays, Wednesdays and Fridays.

Subject to alteration without notice and to weather and circumstances permitting

Page Fifty-four

Royal Route timetable from summer 1935, *Columba*'s last season showing the time-honoured 7:11 departure from Glasgow. By this time the Ardrishaig to Oban sector was covered by a bus service.

Two
David MacBrayne
1879-1905

S.S. CLAYMORE AT OBAN.

The first steamer to enter service for David MacBrayne after he took over the company in his own name in 1879 was *Claymore* in 1881. She is seen here in Oban Bay.

Claymore operated the year-round Glasgow to Stornoway service, along with *Clansman*. Her passenger accommodation was such that this was offered as what would today be termed a mini-cruise. (QRC).

Entrance to Portree Harbour, Skye

Claymore approaching Portree, with a herd of sheep on the hillside above her.

S.S. "Claymore" at Gairloch Pier

Claymore also sailed to Gairloch, and is seen here at Gairloch pier.

Claymore was also painted briefly with a grey hull in 1929.

Claymore, with grey hull, at the North Pier, Oban on 12 July 1929, with, to the right, the Sound of Mull mail boat *Lochinvar*, in her 'exhaust pipes' condition. *Claymore* was sold on 5 May 1931 and was broken up at Bo'ness in the Firth of Forth. The pier buildings seen here were removed in 2002, seventy-five years after they were built.

Cavalier was built for the Glasgow to Inverness service in 1883 by Aitken and Mansel and was to the maximum permissible length for the locks in the Caledonian Canal. In 1919 she was sold to the 'North Company', the North of Scotland, Orkney and Shetland Steam Navigation Co. Ltd., and renamed *Fetlar*. After only a year she was sold to the Dundalk and Newry Steam Packet Co. Ltd., and was used on Irish Sea cattle services until scrapped in 1927.

Cavalier in Neptune's Staircase at Banavie.

Grenadier at Iona, showing the small open boats used to tender to her there. She is seen here with the narrow funnels with which she was fitted when built.

Grenadier was requisitioned by the Admiralty in July 1916 and served as the minesweeper HMS *Grenade*. (CRSC).

Grenadier was built by J.&G. Thomson in 1885, and operated in her initial season from Oban to Gairloch, but spent the remainder of her career on the summer Staffa and Iona route from Oban and as winter relief for the *Columba*. She is seen here in here later years with her new larger funnels going astern out of Oban.

Whilst berthed at Oban's North Pier on the night of 5 September 1927, *Grenadier* was seriously damaged by fire and sank. Captain McArthur, who had commanded her for many years and was semi-retired, and two other crew members were killed. She was towed to Ardrossan on 10 May 1928 and was scrapped there.

The first *Lochness* had been built at the *Lochgoil* in 1853 by J. Barr, and later served on Lough Foyle as the *Lough Foyle*, and then back on the Clyde on the Gareloch. She was purchased by MacBrayne in 1885 for the Loch Ness mail service, and operated on this until scrapped in 1912. (QRC).

Lochness approaching Invermoriston pier.

The *Ethel* had been built by Workman, Clarke at Belfast for County Antrim owners in 1881. She was briefly under the French flag as *Obokh*, and was purchased by MacBraynes in 1885 for the Glasgow to Inverness service. She is seen here, berthed inside *Fusilier* at Ballachulish. In 1910 she was renamed *Clansman*. She was sold in 1916 and sank at sea in October 1924.

Handa had been built as the *Aros Castle* in 1878. In 1887 she was purchased by MacBrayne from Martin Orme, and operated on the cargo services from Glasgow to Tobermory and Loch Sunart, from Oban to Coll and Tiree, and from Portree to Harris. Her small size meant she could sail through the Crinan Canal. She was sold in 1917 to T.W. Ward Ltd, and abandoned at sea, presumably en route to the breakers yard. She is seen here at Black Mill Bay on the island of Luing.

Handa discharging cargo into a small boat at the head of Loch Sunart.

Alex Stephen & Son at Kelvinhaugh had built *Countess of Kellie* in 1869 as a paddle steamer for a ferry service from Alloa to South Alloa across the River Forth. She came into the MacBrayne fleet in 1887 and was converted to screw propulsion and is seen here on the Clyde alongside the *Cavalier*. In mid-stream is an the paddle tug *Fairweather*, which was better known at Aberdeen, and to the far right *Clutha* No.12, later to become MacBrayne's *Lochness*. Behind her is another unidentified *Clutha*. In 1904 she was sold and in 1934 converted to a mooring hulk.

In November 1887 David MacBrayne purchased the deep seas cargo ship *Gladiator*, not illustrated, which had been built for T.&J. Harrison of Liverpool in 1860. She was engaged in ocean tramping and was lost on 12 December 1893 by stranding on the Caberos Shoal whilst en route from Mauritius to London. (GEL).

Opposite below: Fusilier was built in 1888 by McArthur & Co. of Paisley with a single cylinder diagonal engine from Hutson and Corbett. She was built for the Oban to Gairloch service, but soon settled as an Oban-based steamer, serving mainly on the Fort William route. During the latter part of the First World War she was chartered to the Caledonian Steam Packet Co. for service from Wemyss Bay. She is seen here arriving at Ardgour.

Udea was a small coaster acquired in 1888 by David MacBrayne. Schlesinger, Davis & Co. of Newcastle had built her in 1873 for a south Wales colliery. She served MacBraynes as relief cargo steamer and also as a coaling steamer at the smaller ports, and was wrecked in 1894 on the Isle of Gigha. She is seen here with *Iona* at the old pier at Ardrishaig. (GEL).

Fusilier, as built, at Ballachulish pier in a postcard view.

In 1926 *Fusilier*'s funnel was heightened, her bridge was moved forward of the funnel, and a deckhouse added aft of the funnel. She is seen here in Rothsay Bay whilst on the Tarbert run.

Following the loss of the *Grenadier*, *Fusilier* was placed on the Staffa and Iona run in the summers of 1928 to 1930. She is seen here off Staffa on 13 July 1929.

Fusilier refitting prior to the summer season of 1926 in Lamont's yard at Greenock, with the former GSWR turbine *Atalanta* aft of her and CSP turbine *Duchess of Argyll* in dry dock.

In 1934 *Fusilier* was sold to Redcliffe Shipping Co. Ltd. of Hull. She served in the Firth of Forth in that season, and from Llandudno under the name *Lady Orme* in the following season. 1936 saw her running out of Ramsgate, 1937 back at Llandudno, and in 1938 she was renamed *Crestawave*. In October 1939 she was sold for scrapping. This illustration shows her as *Lady Orme* in 1935 with white hull.

GLASGOW, TARBERT, and ARDRISHAIG

BY THE ROYAL MAIL STEAMER

"IONA."

TARBERT.

DAILY at 1.30 p.m. on and after 16th JUNE.

	P.M.		A.M.
Glasgow, ... 1 30		Ardrishaig, ... 6 20	
Partick, ... 1 45		Tarbert, ... 7 5	
Edinburgh, West Princes Street, .. 1 5		Ardlamont, ... 7 50	
Glasgow, Central (Ex.), ... 2 40		Auchinlochan, ... 8 8	
Greenock, C. H. Pier, ... 5 27		Tighnabruaich, ... 8 15	
Glasgow, St. Enoch (Ex.), ... 2 40		Colintraive, ... 8 30	
Greenock, Princes Pier, ... 3 37		Rothesay, ... 9 0	
Kirn, ... 4 2		Innellan, ... 9 27	
Dunoon, ... 4 10		Dunoon, ... 9 45	
Innellan, ... 4 28		Do., N.B. Steamer, .. dep. 10 0	
Rothesay, ... 4 55		Glasgow, Queen Street, .. arr. 11 35	
Colintraive, ... 5 25		Edinburgh, Waverley, ... 2 10	
Tighnabruaich, ... 5 42		Kirn, ... 9 53	
Auchinlochan, ... 5 50		Princes Pier, ...10 18	
Ardlamont, ... 6 7		Do., Express, ... dep. 10 25	
Tarbert, ... 6 45		Glasgow, St. Enoch, .. arr. 11 15	
Ardrishaig, ... 7 30		Edinburgh, via Bellgrove, .. arr. 1 20	
		Custom House Pier, ...10 26	
		C. R. Express, :. .. dep. 10 30	
		Glasgow, Central, ... arr. 11 15	
		Edinburgh, West Princes Street, .. 1 45	
		Partick, ...11 57	
		Glasgow, ...12 10	

Return Tickets available by "COLUMBA" or the "IONA."

AFTERNOON SAIL—GLASGOW TO KIRN,

with the "IONA," and back with the "COLUMBA."

CABIN, 1s. 6d. ; or CABIN, including Dinner, ... 3s. 6d.
FORE CABIN, 1s. 3d. ; or FORE CABIN, including Dinner, ... 2s. 6d.

An 1888 advert for David MacBrayne in 'Pollok's Dictionary of the Clyde' featuring an

afternoon sailing from Glasgow to Ardrishaig by *Iona* and various other offerings.

Pelican had been built at Cork in 1850 for The City of Cork Steam Packet Co. by Ebenezer Pike, who was also the chairman of the shipping company. She had served on the Cork to London and Cork to Bristol Channel services and was purchased by David MacBrayne in September 1888 for a proposed new service from Oban, Glasgow and Liverpool to Iceland. In 1894 she was converted to a coal hulk, first at Portree, and then at Tobermory, being wrecked the following year on Calve Island in a storm (GEL).

"FALCON," BUILT IN CORK, 1854.

Falcon was the sister of *Pelican*, built in 1854 for the same company at the same yard. She was purchased at the same time and placed on tramping work. She sank en route from Glasgow to the United States in December 1890. (GEL).

Texa had been built in 1884 by Scott of Bowling for the Islay cargo service, and was purchased in 1889. She spent some time on the Glasgow to Loch Fyne cargo service after 1900, and is seen here at Ardrishaig. She was sold in 1917 and wrecked in 1932. In 1889 MacBrayne purchased the cargo steamer *Loanda* of 1870, not illustrated, complete with a cargo of coal. She was stationed off Broadford as a floating coal depot, making occasional trips to Hamburg to refill with coal. She was later at Oban, and was scrapped in 1907(GEL).

Tobermory Hotel and Pier

Flowerdale, seen here at Tobermory, had been built as the salvage vessel *Recovery* in 1878 at Barrow. In 1889 she was bought by David MacBrayne and operated to the Outer Islands. She was MacBrayne's first twin-screw steamer and when lost off Lismore in 1904 her engines were salvaged and one each fitted in the new *Plover* and *Cygnet*.

The second *Mountaineer* had begun her life on the Clyde as *Hero* in 1858, built by T. Wingate & Co. Ltd. She had also operated at Belfast and on the Tay. In 1890 David MacBrayne obtained her, and in 1892 she was rebuilt with a clipper bow and bowsprit, and renamed *Mountaineer*. She served mainly on short excursions out of Oban, and was sold in 1909 for scrap. Seen here arriving at Onich. (GEL).

A third *Islay* was purchased in 1890. She had started life on the Stranraer to Larne route as *Princess Louise* in 1872, built by Tod & McGregor. She replaced her predecessor of the same name on the route from Glasgow to Islay and is seen here at Port Askaig. She was lost after stranding on 15 July 1902 on a rock near Sheep Island, Port Ellen.

Lovedale was another of the series of second-hand steamers purchased by MacBrayne at that time. She had been *The Great Western* on 1867, built by Simons of Renfrew for the Great Western Railway, operating from Milford to Waterford and, from 1878 onwards, from Weymouth to Cherbourg. Purchased in 1891, she initially operated from Strome Ferry to Stornoway. In 1893 she was altered and a single funnel replaced her original two. In 1897 on the opening of the railway to Kyle of Lochalsh her sailings were transferred to operate from the latter pier at the opening of which she is seen here, dressed overall. In 1904 she briefly operated from Glasgow to Islay and was scrapped the following year.

Gael had been built in 1867 for the Campbeltown & Glasgow Steam Packet Joint Stock Co. Ltd, by Robertson & Co. with machinery by Rankin and Blackmore, both of Greenock. She had been sold in 1883 to the Great Western Railway Co. for their new Weymouth to Cherbourg service. She ran in the Bristol Channel in 1885 and 1886 and was chartered to run from Penzance to the Scilly Isles in 1887. David MacBrayne purchased her in 1891 and she was placed on the Oban to Gairloch service, and is seen here at Portree in a postcard view.

In 1919, with a number of CSP steamers still not returned from war service, *Gael* was chartered by the CSP, and is seen here in that guise, approaching Dunoon. In May 1924 she was sold for breaking up.

Brigadier was the third Weymouth-based steamer in a row to be purchased by David MacBrayne. She had been built in 1854 as the *Cygnus* for the Weymouth & Channel Islands Steam Packet Co. Ltd and came to Scotland in 1891, being placed on the Loch Fyne cargo service. Around 1892 she was rebuilt and renamed *Brigadier*. As well as serving the Loch Fyne route, she operated from Oban to Loch Sunart, and relieved *Lochiel* on the Outer Isles service from Portree. Whilst on the latter service she was wrecked near Rodel, Harris, on 7 December 1896.

Carabinier, seen here arriving at Oban Railway Pier, had been built at Southampton for the London & South Western, and London, Brighton, & South Coast Railway's joint service from Portsmouth to the Isle of Wight in 1878 as *Albert Edward*. Purchased by MacBrayne's in 1893, she served on the Oban-Sound of Mull-Tobermory-Loch Sunart service, and was sold for scrapping in 1908. (GEL)

Gairlochy had previously been the Clyde steamer *Sultan* of 1861, sailing from 1862 to 1891 for Capt. Alexander Williamson, then briefly for the Glasgow & South Western Railway, and from 1893 for Capt. John Williamson as *Ardmore*. In late 1894 she was purchased by David MacBrayne and renamed *Gairlochy* for service on the Caledonian Canal, running opposite the *Gondolier*.

On 24 December 1919, *Gairlochy* was destroyed by fire at Fort Augustus, and was subsequently dismantled, and her hull sunk, where it can still be seen when the water in the loch is low.

The *Glendale* had been built for the London, Brighton and South Coast Railway by John Elder & Co. at Govan in 1875 as the *Paris* for the Newhaven to Dieppe service. In 1888 she was sold back to Fairfields, as Elders were now known as, and from 1890 to 1892 ran from Liverpool to North Wales. From 1892 to 1895 she operated from Hamburg to Helgoland for Albert Ballin, and from 1896 to 1902 for W M Rhodes of London from Tilbury to Ostend as *La Belgique*. In 1902 she was purchased by David MacBrayne and named *Glendale*. She worked on various routes including that from Glasgow to Islay. Whilst on this service, on 20 July 1905, she was wrecked off the Mull of Kintyre as seen in this illustration.

Lapwing was the first of a batch of three sister ships to be built. Delivered from Scotts of Bowling in 1903 she operated on the Outer Islands mail service from Oban, and, from 1908 from Portree to the Outer Islands, returning to Dunvegan. She stranded on 28 January 1917 on Rat Rock, Oban, and after being salved, was sold to Clyde Cargo Steamers who renamed her *Cowal* and operated her until scrapping in 1931. She is seen here being tendered by a small ferry at Kilchoan.

Sheila was built by A.&J. Inglis in 1904 and was the first vessel in the fleet with triple expansion machinery. She served on the mail service between Kyle of Lochalsh, where she is seen here, and Stornoway in most years until lost in the early hours of New Years Day 1927 by running aground in Cuiag bay, just south of the entrance to Loch Torridon. The losses of 1927 did much to put MacBrayne Company effectively out of business

Plover was built as a sister ship to *Lapwing* in 1904, also by Scotts of Bowling, and was fitted with one boiler and the port engine of the *Flowerdale*. She worked on the Outer Islands services from Oban, Mallaig, and Kyle, and is seen here at Balmacara, near Kyle, beached to have her bottom cleaned and painted.

In 1934, the *Plover* was altered to become the Directors' yacht and was renamed *Loch Aline*. She was also used as a winter relief vessel and on occasional excursions from Oban. During the Second World War she was requisitioned and used as an examination vessel at Rothesay from 1940 to 1945. She was sold after the war to Burns & Laird Lines and again in 1947 to Dublin owners who used her as a cargo steamer again. She was scrapped in 1951.

Cygnet, the third of the *Lapwing* trio, came from A.&J. Inglis in 1904, and had the starboard engine from the *Flowerdale* and the other boiler. She was purely a cargo steamer, and was initially employed on the Glasgow to Loch Fyne cargo service with winter reliefs on the Outer Islands services. She had very little passenger accommodation. From 1919 she was permanently on the Outer Islands service from Oban, where she is seen here at the Railway Pier, to Coll, Tiree, Castlebay and Lochboisdale. *Cygnet* was sold in 1930 for scrapping at Barrow.

Brenda, seen here to the left at Kinlochleven, came from Scotts of Bowling in 1904 and had a second-hand engine from an 1888-built yacht. The boiler had been the donkey-engine boiler on the *Flowerdale*. She was small enough to pass through the Crinan Canal, and ran along with the *Handa* on the Glasgow to Mull and Glasgow to Inverness cargo runs. She was scrapped in 1929 at Troon. Behind her is a Kelly coaster.

Pioneer, the penultimate paddle steamer to be built for the Company, came from A.&J. Inglis in 1905 and was built for the Islay Mail service from West Loch Tarbert. She is seen here arriving at Port Askaig with a good load of passengers and the hills of Jura in the background.

Pioneer at West Loch Tarbert. She worked the Islay service until 1940, by which time she was the last paddle steamer in the MacBrayne fleet, and subsequently operated on various services from Oban. (CRSC)

Pioneer arriving at Port Askaig, with the Paps of Jura in the background.

Pioneer was requisitioned by the Admiralty in 1944. She was used, stationed off Fairlie, as the HQ of submarine control for the North Atlantic, and in 1945 was purchased by the Admiralty and renamed HMS *Harbinger*. From 1946 until scrapped in 1958 her hull, with paddles and sponsons removed, was used as a floating laboratory in Portland Harbour. She is seen here at Portland as HMS *Harbinger*. (AA).

The second *Clydesdale* was built in 1905 by Scotts of Bowling for the Glasgow to Inverness cargo trade, and was an almost exact copy of *Cavalier*, with whom she originally ran. After the loss of *Glendale*, she was transferred to the Glasgow to Islay cargo run. From 1927, following the loss of the *Sheila*, until the advent of the *Lochness* in 1929, she performed the Stornoway mail run, and was also on the Glasgow to Stornoway service in the winter months. (QRC).

Clydesdale at Oban in her later years, after a wheelhouse had been fitted. She was latterly used to carry sheep from the islands to Oban and Kyle, and was sold in 1953 for scrapping at Port Glasgow.

Three
David MacBrayne Ltd
1905-1928

1907-1909 saw the introduction of three paraffin-engined motor vessels by what was now David MacBrayne Ltd. The first of these was *Comet*, which had been built in London two years previously by A.W. Robertson of Canning Town as *Win*. It is probable that she served as a motor yacht on the Thames. She commenced service with the company on the route from Ballachulish to Kinlochleven. In 1919 she operated in connection with the *Columba* from Ardrishaig to Inveraray, but she was, in the main, used in the Lochgoilhead service until withdrawn in 1946.

After withdrawal, *Comet* was sold to owners as Shoreham, where she was renamed *Gradley* She may have operated short cruises on a few occasions, but was soon converted to a houseboat at Shoreham, where she remains to this day. She is seen here in a photograph taken in July 2000.

The second motor vessel of 1907 was the *Scout*. Built by Ailsa at Troon, she served the Ballachulish to Kinlochleven service until destroyed by fire on 19 August 1913. She is seen here at Oban, possibly in June 1909 when she deputised for *Lochinvar* on the Sound of Mull mail service.

The third vessel to join the fleet in 1907 was the magnificent *Chieftain*, built to replace the *Clansman* of 1870 on the Glasgow to Stornoway service. She was the first vessel owned by MacBraynes to exceed 1,000 tons. (QRC).

Chieftain was sold in 1919 to the North of Scotland, Orkney & Shetland Steam Navigation Co. Ltd. and renamed *St Margaret*. She is seen here at St Margaret's Hope in Orkney. In 1925 she was sold to the Canadian National Steam Ship Co. Ltd and renamed *Prince Charles* for use on the British Columbia Coastal services, and in 1940 to the Union Steamship Co. of British Columbia, and again renamed *Camosun*. In 1945 she was sold for use as a blockade-runner transporting refugees to Palestine, now named *Cairo*, and was yet again sold in 1947, to trade between Marseilles and Beira. In 1952 she was scrapped at La Spezia.

The third of the three motor vessels mentioned above was *Lochinvar*, the only one large enough to be thought of as a ship. She was a triple screw vessel, with three paraffin engines, and entered service in 1908 on the Oban to Tobermory mail service, replacing *Carabinier*. She originally appeared with no funnel, but later three exhaust pipes, one for each of the three engines, were fitted as seen here.

After the exhaust pies were removed she was fitted with a single tall funnel, as seen in this postcard view of her at Oban Railway Pier.

Lochinvar was re-engined in 1926 and 1949 and, in the latter year was converted to twin screw. By that time she had a regular funnel. She is seen here approaching Tobermory, with *Lochgarry* in the background.

Lochinvar at Tobermory, terminus of the Sound of Mull mail service, on 12 August 1954, her last year employed full time on that route. The pier building, clearly shown, was of art deco style and built in the 1930s.

At the same time as her 1949 re-engining, *Lochinvar* received a wheelhouse and, in 1952, a mainmast. She was a spare vessel from 1955 onwards, and in 1959 was placed on the Portree mail run. She is seen here at Mallaig in 1959. (QRC).

In June 1960 *Lochinvar* was sold and from 1961 to 1963 operated as *Anzio I* on the Thames from Sheerness to Southend. In 1966 she was sold to Scottish owners to run from Inverness, but whilst on her delivery voyage northwards, was wrecked south of the Humber with the loss of all on board. (QRC).

A second *Lochiel* appeared from Scott's of Bowling in 1908. She was fitted with a gyroscope to stop rolling. She ran on the route from Mull to the Outer Islands and was taken over by the Admiralty on 12 January 1917 and was blown up in July 1918 while acting as a fleet runner in the Bristol Channel. The small cargo steamer *Nellie*, built in 1892, not illustrated, was purchased in 1908, renamed *Staffa* in 1910, and was sold in 1916. She was finally in Guernsey ownership and was lost around 1947.

The small cargo steamer *Dirk* was built in 1909 by Scott of Bowling to operate a variety of cargo services based at Tobermory, serving Coll, Tiree, and Bunessan. She was taken up for war service in 1915 as an armed escort vessel and was torpedoed off Flamborough Head on 28 May 1918. (GEL).

The final paddle steamer to be built for MacBrayne was the *Mountaineer* of 1910. She came from A.&J. Inglis of Pointhouse. Similar to *Pioneer*, but with the promenade deck not carried forward to the bow, she was used on various routes out of Oban, including those to Fort William, Tobermory, relieving the *Lochinvar*, and Crinan. She also, on occasion, relieved the *Pioneer* on the Islay mail service, the *Fusilier* on the Portree mail service, and the *Comet* on the Lochgoilhead route. *Mountaineer* was scrapped at Port Glasgow in September 1938.

In 1911 MacBrayne took over the Loch Leven Shipping Co. Ltd., which operated, from Ballachulish to Kinlochleven, where an aluminium smelter had been built in 1904. Along with the purchase came two vessels, the *Loch Leven Queen*, illustrated here, and the small motorboat *Cona*. Russell & Co. of Port Glasgow had built *Loch Leven Queen* in 1896 for inner-city service in Glasgow as *Clutha No.12*, and she had later sailed on Lough Neagh as *Lough Neagh Queen*. She had come to the West Highlands in 1908 and in 1912, was transferred by MacBraynes to the Loch Ness mail service, being renamed *Lochness* and replacing the first vessel of that name. She was sold in 1929 for scrapping at Inverness.

In 1914 the *Countess of Mayo* joined the MacBrayne fleet. Seath of Rutherglen had built her for the River Shannon Development Co. in 1897, in whose colours she is seen here. In 1908 she had been sold to operate excursions on Carlingford Lough from Warrenpoint. MacBrayne operated her on the Ballachulish to Kinlochleven service and she was sold in 1917 for use on the Cromarty to Invergordon ferry and in 1919 she was purchased by Hawthorn Leslie and renamed *Walker* for Tyne ferry service. She was broken up in 1947.

A steamer named *Duke of Abercorn* (not illustrated) was purchased from Dublin owners at the same time, but never operated for MacBrayne and was sold for scrapping the following year. She had been built as *Britannia* for service from Morecambe in 1888. (GEL).

In 1920 a third *Lochiel*, seen to the right here, entered the fleet. She had been built in 1906 by Scott of Kinghorn for Guernsey owners as *Devonia*, for a cargo/passenger service from Plymouth to Guernsey and St Briac. She served mainly on the Glasgow to Stornoway cargo service and was withdrawn in February 1937 and sold the following year, back to the Channel Islands, where she was renamed *Isle Of Alderney*. She was taken over by another company in 1940 and took part in the evacuation of the Channel Islands, going to Greek owners in 1946 as *Annoula* and to Panama flag owners later that year as *Monte Lirio*, being scrapped in 1954. Astern of her in this photograph at Oban North Pier is *Loch Aline*, ex *Plover*. (QRC).

A Thames motor lighter owned by Crosse and Blackwell, named C.&B. No.1, which had been built in 1913 at Ipswich, was purchased in 1928 for a feeder service from Bowmore to various distillery piers on Islay. She was renamed *Lochgorm* in 1930 and is seen here at Bowmore *c*.1929, still as *C.&B. No.1*. (AA).

In 1936 *Lochgorm* was named *Iona* to preserve the famous name for future MacBrayne use on a more eminent vessel. In 1937 she was replaced by road transport and withdrawn from service. She was sold to the Ardrossan Dockyard Ltd in the following year and the hull used as a painter's platform. (AA).

Four
New Ownership
1928-1947

The first evidence of the Coast Lines connection in the new jointly owned company was in the purchase of this steamer, which became the first *Lochdunvegan*. Cairds had built her in 1891 as the *Grouse* for G.&J. Burns. In 1922 she had been sold to Grahamston Shipping Co. Ltd. and renamed *Kelvindale*. Coast Lines later absorbed this company and in 1924 she was transferred to Coast Lines Ltd as *Denbigh Coast*. She mainly served on the weekly direct Glasgow to Stornoway cargo service, calling only at Tobermory and Portree. She was withdrawn in 1948 and was sold for scrapping at Faslane. Seen here off Tobermory

The first of the four new vessels to appear, and the only one to be a steamer, was *Lochness*, built by Harland & Wolff at Govan for the Stornoway mail run to replace the *Sheila*. She made her maiden voyage from Glasgow to Tarbert on Glasgow Fair Saturday 1929 and entered service on her intended route on 1 August of that year. She served the route from Mallaig and Kyle to Stornoway until 1947. She is seen here at Kyle of Lochalsh at Easter 1930 with the grey hull with which she originally served.

After replacement by *Loch Seaforth* in 1947, *Lochness* was placed on the Outer Islands service from Oban whilst *Lochearn* was re-engined and was then was spare steamer for a number of years. She is seen here at Kyle of Lochalsh on June 1953, dressed overall for the Coronation. (H.Townley).

In 1955 *Lochness* was sold to an Italian operator and was named *Valmarina*, and in 1958 to Greek owners, for whom she served as *Myrtidiotissa* serving the Aegean islands for a number of years. She was still in service in 1970 and was broken up in 1974. (QRC).

The cargo motorship *Lochshiel* was also built in 1929, by Henry Robb of Leith. She was built to replace *Brenda* on the cargo run from Glasgow to Mull, Loch Sunart, and Loch Leven. Being a larger vessel, she could not, of course, use the Crinan Canal. She was sold in 1952 and broken up in Belgium a couple of years later. Seen here at Anderston Quay, Glasgow – *Waverley's* current berth. (QRC).

STEAMER SERVICES.

ARDRISHAIG MAIL STEAMER (with Connection for Oban)

P.S. "Fusilier"

Daily (except Sundays).

	Until 31st Oct. and from 1st Apr.	From 1st Nov. till 31st M'rch			Until 31st Oct. and from 1st Apr.	From 1st Nov. till 31st M'rch
	a.m.	a.m.			p.m.	p.m.
Glasgow (St. En.)...tr. dep.	7§30	7§30	Ardrishaig ...str. dep.		1 0	1 30
Greenock (Prin. Pr.) str. ,,	9 0	9 0	Tarbert ,, ,,		1 40	2 20
Edinburgh (Pr. St.) tr. ,,	6§20	6§20	Tighnabruaich ,, ,,		2 40	3 25
Glasgow (Central)... ,,	8§35	8§35	Colintraive ,, ,,		2 55	3 40
Gourock ...str.	9 28	9 28	Rothesay ,, ,,		3 30	4 15
Edinburgh (Wav.) tr. ,,	6§25	6§25	Innellan ,, ,,		3 50	4 45
Glasgow (Queen St.) ,,	7§55	7§55	Dunoon ,, ,,		4 10	5 0
Dunoon ...str.	9 45	9 50	Glasgow (Queen St.) tr. arr.		§6*36	...
Innellan ,,	9 55	10 10	Edinburgh (Wav.) ,,		§9*28	...
Rothesay ,,	10 15	10 40	Gourock ...str.		4 25	5 25
Colintraive ,,	10 40	11 10	Glasgow (Central) ...tr.		5§47	c6§56
Tighnabruaich ,,	10 55	11 25	Edinburgh (Pr. St.)... ,,		8§10	10§47
Tarbert (for Islay).... ,,	11 55	1230p	Greenock (Prin. Pr.)..str.		4 45	5 40
Ardrishaig ,, arr.	1240p	1 20	Glasgow (St. En.)....tr. ,,		6§18	7§18

c 7.11 on Saturdays.   * Saturdays only.
§ Subject to alteration—See Railway Time Tables.

CONNECTING (Motor Road) SERVICE WITH OBAN

Daily (except Sundays)

	Until 31st Oct. & from 1st April	Until 31st Oct.	From 1st Nov. till 31st Mar		Until 31st Oct.	From 1st Oct.
	p.m.	p.m.	p.m.		a.m.	a.m.
Ardrishaig..car. dep.	1 0	1 10	1 45	Oban......car. dep.	10 35	9 0
Oban...... ,, arr.	4 50	3 25	5 50	Ardrishaig.. ,, arr.	12 45p	12 40p

ISLAY MAIL STEAMER

P.S. "Pioneer"

	Mon., Wed., Fri.	Tues., Thur., Sat.		Mon., Wed., Fri.	Tues., Thur., Sat.
	p.m.	p.m.		a.m.	a.m.
Tarbert, W.......str. dep.	12 50	12 50	Port Ellen ....str. dep.	8 30	...
Gigha ,, ,,	...	2 30	Gigha ,, ,,	10 10	...
Port Ellen ,, arr.	...	4 25	Port Askaig ,, ,,	...	8 30
Jura ,, dep.	3 30	...	Jura ,, ,,	...	9 30
Port Askaig ,, arr.	4 25	...	Tarbert, W......... ,, arr.	11 30	11 30

LOCHGOIL MAIL STEAMER

T.S.S. "Comet"

Daily (except Sundays).

	a.m.			p.m.
Glasgow Central...tr. dep.	8§35	Lochgoilhead ...str. dep.		12 40
St. Enoch ,,	7§30	Douglas Pier ,, ,,		12 48
Greenock (Princes Pier)..str. ,,	9 0	Carrick Castle ,, ,,		1 10
Gourock ,, ,,	9 35	Cove ,, ,,		2 * 0
Kilcreggan ,, ,,	...	Kilcreggan ,, ,,		2 15
Cove ,, ,,	...	Gourock ,, arr.		2 25
Carrick Castle ,, ,,	10 50	Glasgow (Central) ...tr. arr.		3§46
Douglas Pier ,, ,,	11 12	Greenock (Princes Pier)..str. ,,		2 40
Lochgoilhead ,, arr.	11 20	Glasgow (St. Enoch) ...tr. ,,		b4§28

* Saturdays only.   b 4.17 on Saturdays.
§ Subject to alteration—See Railway Time Tables.

The time ... particulars stated above are for general information and are

Pages from the winter 1929-30 timetable, annotated, probably by C.L.D. Duckworth, with the relevant operating steamers. Note that at that time the winter Ardrishaig service commenced at Greenock Princes Pier and the Inner and Outer Islands services were in the form in which

STEAMER SERVICES.

OBAN AND LISMORE STEAMER.

	Wednesdays only.			Weds. only.
	a.m.	p.m.		a.m.
Oban ....dep.	11 0	3 0	Lismore........... dep.	11 50
Lismore ....arr.	11 40	3 40	Oban...........arr.	12 30p

OBAN, LISMORE, SOUND OF MULL AND TOBERMORY STEAMER.
Daily (except Sundays).

T.S.S "Lochinvar." T.S. "Mountaineer."

	Weds. only.	Except Weds.		Until 12th Oct.	From 14th Oct.
	a.m.	a.m.		a.m.	a.m.
Glasgow (Bu. St.)..tr. dep.	8 §0	8 §0	Tobermory.........str. dep.	7 15	7 30
Oban ....str. ,,	3 0p	1 15p	Drimnin .... ,, ,,	7 40	7 55
Lismore .... ,, ,,	3 40	...	Salen, Mull......... ,, ,,	8 20	8 35
Craignure .... ,, ,,	4 30	2 5	Lochaline .... ,, ,,	8 55	9 10
Lochaline .... ,, ,,	5 0	2 35	Craignure .... ,, ,,	9 25	9 40
Salen, Mull ...... ,, ,,	5 35	3 10	Oban .... ,, ,,	10 15	10 30
Drimnin .... ,, ,,	6 15	3 50	Glasgow (Bu. St.) tr. arr.	4 38p	4 38p
Tobermory ...... ,, arr.	6 40	4 15			

§ Subject to alteration—See Railway Time Tables.

INNER ISLANDS STEAMER.

S.S. "Cygnet."

	Mons. & Weds.		Fridays
	a.m.		a.m.
Oban...........dep.	6 0	Oban ....dep.	6 0
Tobermory .... ,,	8 45	Tobermory............... ,,	8 45
Kilchoan .... ,,	9 30	Kilchoan .... ,,	9 30
Coll .... ,,	11 30	Coll............... ,,	11 30
Tiree .... ,,	1 0p	Tiree .... ,,	1 0p
Castlebay .... arr.	6 0	Castlebay ....arr.	6 0
Lochboisdale .... ,,	8 30	Castlebay ....dep.	7 0
Lochboisdale ....dep.	9 30	Canna .... ,,	11 30
Castlebay ....arr.	12 0nt		

	Tues. & Thurs.		Sats.
	a.m.		a.m.
Castlebay ....dep.	3 0	Tiree ....dep.	5 30
Tiree .... ,,	8 30	Coll........... ,,	7 0
Coll .... ,,	9 30	Kilchoan .... ,,	8 30
Kilchoan .... ,,	11 0	Tobermory........... ,,	9 15
Tobermory .... ,,	12 1p	Oban ....arr.	12 1p
Oban...........arr.	3 0		

OUTER ISLANDS STEAMER.

S.S. "Plover."

	Mons.		Weds.	Fris.
	a.m.		a.m.	a.m.
Kyle ....dep.	9 0	Kyle ....dep.	6 0	6 0
Glenelg .... ,,	9 45	Scalpay........... ,,	11 30	11 30
Armadale .... ,,	10 45	Tarbert........... ,,	12 30p	12 30p
Mallaig ....arr.	11 15	Stockinish .... ,,	1 30	No Call.
Mallaig ....dep.	1 0p	Rodel........... ,,	2 30	2 30
Eigg .... ,,	2 30	Lochmaddy .... ,,	4 30	4 30
Rum .... ,,	4 0	Dunvegan .... ,,	No Call.	7 45
Canna .... ,,	5 0	Lochboisdale...........arr.	7 30	11 55
Lochboisdale........... ,,	9 0			
Lochmaddy...........arr.	11 59			

	Tues.		Thurs.	Sats.
	a.m.		a.m.	a.m.
Lochmaddy...........dep.	5 0	Lochboisdale...........dep.	3 0	12 15
Rodel .... ,,	7 0	Canna .... ,,	7 0	...
Tarbert........... ,,	9 0	Rum........... ,,	8 0	...
Scalpay .... ,,	9 45	Eigg .... ,,	9 30	...
Kyle ....arr.	3 15p	Mallaig ....arr.	11 0	6 15
		Mallaig ....dep.	12 30p	12 30p
		Armadale .... ,,	1 10	1 10
		Glenelg .... ,,	2 30	2 30
		Kyle ....arr.	3 30	3 30

they would be continued by *Lochearn* and *Lochmor* until the commencement of the car ferry era in 1964 (GEL).

STEAMER SERVICES.

MALLAIG, KYLE OF LOCHALSH, AND PORTREE STEAMER
Daily (except Sundays) :—

P.S. "Glencoe".

	Until 31st Oct.	From 1st Nov.			Until 31st Oct.	From 1st Nov.
	a.m.	a.m.			a.m.	a.m.
Glasgow (Qn. St)........tr. dep.	5 §45	5 §50	Portree ....str. dep.		7 0	7 0
Mallaig........str. ,,	12 0n	12 0n	Raasay .... ,, ,,		7 50	7 50
Kyle .... ,, arr.	2 0p	2 0p	Broadford............ ,, ,,		8 40	8 40
			Kyle .... ,, arr.		9 30	9 30
Glasgow (Cen.) tr. dep.	4 §15a	4 §15a	Glasgow (Bu. St.)......tr. ,,		9§24p	9§24p
Kyle............str. ,,	2 45p	2 45p				
Broadford. .... ,, ,,	3 25	3 25	Kyle...................str. dep.		9 35a	9 35a
Raasay .... ,, ,,	4 25	4 25	Mallaig............ ,, arr.		11 30	11 30
Portree .... ,, arr.	5 45	5 45	Glasgow (Qn. St.)......tr. arr.		5§44p	5§44p

§ Subject to alteration—See Railway Time Tables.

MALLAIG, KYLE OF LOCHALSH, AND STORNOWAY STEAMER

T.S.S. "Lochness".

	Except Suns. Until 31st October.	Except Suns. From 1st Nov.			Except Sats. Until 31st Oct.	Except Sats. From 1st Nov.
	a.m.	a.m.			p.m.	p.m.
Glasgow (Qn. St).tr. dep.	5 §45	5 §50	Stornoway......str. dep.		11 0	11 0
Mallaig........str. ,,	12 0n	12 0n	Applecross...... ,, ,,		3 15a	...
Kyle .... ,, arr.	B2 0p	B2 0p	Kyle .... ,, arr.		4 15	4 15a
			Glasgow (Bu. St.) tr. ,,		5§15p	5§15p
Glasgow (Cen.) ...tr. dep.	4 §15a	4 §15a	Kyle ....str. dep.		5 45a	6 15
Kyle ....str. ,,	2 15p	2 30p	Glenelg............ ,, ,,		6v25	6v55
Applecross ... ,, ,,	3 5	3 20	Armadale....... ,, ,,		7v15	7v45
Stornoway ... ,, arr.	7 30	7 45	Mallaig .... ,, arr.		7 45	8 15
			Glasgow (Qn. St.) tr. ,,		1§56p	2§12p

B Change at Kyle of Lochalsh.   v Tuesdays, Thursdays, and Saturdays only.
§ Subject to alteration—See Railway Time Tables.

STEAMER FARES

FROM MALLAIG

TO	Single		Return	
	1st Cl.	3rd Cl.	1st Cl.	3rd Cl.
	s. d.	s. d.	s. d.	s. d.
Broadford	7 9	4 6	13 3	7 6
Raasay	11 11	6 1	20 3	10 6
Portree	13 2	6 10	22 3	11 9
Applecross ...	11 1	5 7	19 0	9 6
Stornoway ...	25 4	13 4	43 6	23 9

FROM KYLE OF LOCHALSH

TO	Single		Return	
	1st Cl.	3rd Cl.	1st Cl.	3rd Cl.
	s. d.	s. d.	s. d.	s. d.
Broadford	2 1	1 1	3 6	1 9
Raasay	5 0	2 8	8 3	4 3
Portree	5 6	3 0	9 3	5 3
Applecross ...	3 6	1 9	6 0	3 0
Stornoway ...	17 9	10 0	30 6	17 3

Through Fares from Glasgow
Via MALLAIG or KYLE OF LOCHALSH

TO	Single		
	1st Cl.	3rd Cl. & Cab.	3rd Cl.
	s. d.	s. d.	s. d.
Portree	47 1	33 6	28 3
Stornoway ...	59 3	45 8	34 1

TO	Return		
	1st Cl.	3rd Cl. & Cab.	3rd Cl.
	s. d.	s. d.	s. d.
Portree	94 2	62 11	56 6
Stornoway ...	111 4	84 2	64 5

Children above 3 and under 14 years of age Half-Fare.

The above Fares are subject to revision at any time without notice.

The times and particulars stated above are for general information and are not guaranteed. Subject to alteration without notice and to weather and circumstances permitting

The third page, and the final one with shipping services, from the winter 1929-1930 timetable.

The *Lochearn* was the second of the four new vessels specified in the agreement which formed the new company. A motorship, she was built in 1930, along with sister *Lochmor*, by the Ardrossan Dockyard Ltd, which was then owned by the Kylsant Group who also owned Coast Lines. Both were initially unsatisfactory, giving a speed of around 9 knots instead of the required 12.5 knots. Both vessels were consequently re-engined in 1948. *Lochearn* is seen here in her original grey hull condition at Oban North Pier in June 1931 with *Mountaineer* behind her. (QRC).

Lochearn in Loch Scavaig on the south coast of Skye. A cruise to here from Mallaig was part of the Mallaig-based Outer Islands roster, so she must have been relieving *Lochmor* on this occasion. In this illustration she has the smaller funnel she received after re-engining in 1948.

Lochearn arriving at Oban, from where she maintained the Inner Islands mail service to Tobermory, Coll, Tiree, Castlebay and Lochboisdale until 1955, when she replaced *Lochinvar* on the Sound of Mull mail run. Both *Lochearn* and *Lochmor* operated, carrying crane-loaded cars, from Oban to Craignure and Lochaline in the first weeks of the car ferry timetable in 1964 until the new *Columba* was available. She was sold in 1964 to Greek owners and was renamed *Amimoni*, but appears never to have operated in Greek waters and was probably broken up by the early seventies. (QRC).

Lochmor or *Lochearn*, in all probability the former, in a postcard view of Mallaig (posted in 1933) along with the *Fusilier*. *Lochmor*'s sailings described a circuit of Skye from Mallaig, calling at Kyle, Portree, Tarbert, Rodel, Lochmaddy, Lochboisdale, where she met up with the Oban Inner Islands vessel, normally the *Lochmor*, returning via Canna, Rhum, and Eigg. From 1947 she also operated a Loch Scavaig cruise from Mallaig, with a connecting cargo ferry service in a small boat to Soay incorporated whilst the vessel was anchored in Loch Scavaig and the passengers ashore to explore the remote inland Loch Coruisk. Sold with her sister to Greece she was named *Naias* and was broken up in 1969.

PLEASURE SAILINGS

BY

M.V. "LOCHMOR"

for week commencing Monday, 23rd August

Monday, 23rd August

2-30 p.m. Cruise to ISLES OF THE SEA (Holy Isles). St. Columba's Landing Place. Returning to Oban about 6 p.m. By Sound of Kerrera, passing Kilbowie and Gallanach, Gylen Castle, Easdale and Luing, and affording magnificent views of Mull, Jura and Lorn Mountains.
Return Fare 7/6

Tuesday, 24th August

2-30 p.m. To LOCH CRERAN, due back about 5-30 p.m. Passing Dunollie and Dunstaffnage Castles, viewing Connel Bridge, and Beregonium, Eriska Island, Lismore, and up Loch Creran, viewing Barcaldine Castle and grand scenery on the north side of Loch Creran, and Creagan Narrows.
Return Fare 7/6

6-30 p.m. Cruise to LOCH SPELVIE (MULL), via Sound of Kerrera and Gylen Castle, entering and cruising to head of Loch Spelvie, passing Loch Don, Shepherd's Hat, viewing Duart Castle; Lismore, etc., returning to Oban about 9-30 p.m.
Return Fare 5/-

Wednesday, 25th August

2-30 p.m. CRUISE to LOCH CORRY and Round LISMORE, due back about 5-30 p.m. Passing Dunollie and Dunstaffnage Castles, viewing Connel Bridge and Beregonium, Eriska Island, Lismore, etc.
Return Fare 7/6

6 30 p.m. CRUISE to ISLES OF THE SEA (Holy Isles), St. Columba's landing place, by Sound of Kerrera, passing Kilbownie and Gallanach, Gylen Castle, Easdale and Luing, and affording magnificent views of Mull, Jura, and Lorn Mountains. Due back about 9-30 p.m.
Return Fare 5/-

Thursday, 26th August

10 a.m. EXCURSION to LOCH SPELVIE and SALEN (MULL), allowing passengers about one hour ashore at Salen. Due back about 5 p.m. Steamer passes through Sound of Kerrera, viewing Kilbowie and Gallanach, Gylen Castle, Loch Spelvie, Loch Don, Duart Castle, Ardtornish Castle.
Return Fare 12/-

Friday, 27th August

10-30 a.m. EXCURSION TO CRINAN, allowing passengers about one hour ashore at Crinan. Due back 5 p.m. Steamer passes through Sound of Kerrera, viewing Kilbowie and Gallanach, Gylen Castle, Easdale and Luing, and Strait of Corrievrechan, also Loch Melfort with its archipelago of small isles at the entrance. An excellent view is afforded of the Mull, Jura, and Lorn Mountains.
Return Fare 12/-

Saturday, 28th August

9-30 a.m. EXCURSION to TOBERMORY and LOCH SUNART, due back about 5-30 p.m. Passing Dunollie and Duart Castles, Lady Rock, Torosay and Ardtornish Castles. After leaving Tobermory the Steamer strikes across Auliston Point and ascends the winding reaches of Loch Sunart, past Oronsay Island on the right, and Glenborrodale Castle on the left. Steamer leaves Tobermory on the return journey at 3 p.m.
Return Fare 12/-

☞ The Owners reserve the right to alter or cancel any of these trips as may be found necessary.

All passengers and their luggage and goods and live stock are only carried subject to the conditions specified on back of the Company's General Sailing Bills.

TICKETS MUST BE BOOKED PRIOR TO JOINING VESSEL

AT

D. MacBrayne Ltd., Steam Packet Office,

In summer 1948 *Lochmor* was at Oban, covering for *Lochinvar*, which was on overhaul. In late August she offered a series of short sailings as in this handbill.

Lochmor at Kyle in a post-war view with a turntable car ferry in the foreground. The ferry service from Kyle to Kyleakin, although deep into MacBrayne territory, was actually operated by the Caledonian Steam Packet Co. from 1945 until the formation of Caledonian MacBrayne in 1973. The ferry is probably the *Portree* (1951), *Broadford* (1953) or *Lochalsh* (1957).

The steamer *Lochbroom* had been built as *City of London* for the Aberdeen Steam Navigation Co. Ltd as far back as 1871 by Elders at Govan. Purchased by MacBraynes in 1931 she replaced the *Claymore*, ten years her junior, on the passenger service from Glasgow to Lochinver, occasionally extended to Loch Clash pier in Loch Inchard. She is seen here at the MacBrayne mooring at Lancefield Quay in Glasgow, the current berth of PS *Waverley*. (QRC).

Lochbroom at Tobermory. She was sold for scrapping at Port Glasgow in July 1937. Note – there is no Macbrayne office at the pier.

The fourth vessel from the 1929 contract was the *Lochfyne*, notable in being the first diesel-electric passenger vessel to enter service in British coastal waters. She is seen here, with the grey hull colours which she initially carried, sailing down the Clyde from Glasgow in June 1931, where prior to her entering service with fare-paying passengers, she was on public view for Glasgow Civic Week, along with the *Glencoe*. These were, of course, MacBrayne's oldest and newest vessels. (QRC).

Cover of the 1935 MacBrayne guide and timetable, featuring the *Lochfyne* and a MacBrayne bus.

Lochfyne was placed on the Staffa and Iona service from Oban in summer and served as winter relief vessel on the Ardrishaig mail service. In her early years a series of postcards, of paintings by Gilfillan, were published, in a similar style to this, showing her in grey-hull condition off Fingal's Cave on Staffa. Artistic license shows her considerably nearer than she would actually have sailed.

Lochfyne at Fort William in an early post-war postcard vies with a fleet of MacBrayne buses waiting to take the passengers on to Inverness. The card is prior to 1953 when she received a mainmast. The 1930s art deco pier office and MacBrayne office show well (RB).

Following the introduction of *King George V* in 1936 on the round Mull service, *Lochfyne* was placed on the Oban to Fort William run until 1939. She continued on this route in the early season in post-war years and is seen here leaving Fort William astern on 13 July 1956. (QRC).

Lochfyne at Oban in 1963. From 1958, following the withdrawal of *Saint Columba*, she had run year round on the Tarbert and Ardrishaig mail run, but operated excursion services out of Oban for a few weeks in early summer. (RB).

Pleasure Sailings
and Excursions
THIS WEEK

from

MacBrayne's Pier, Fort William

Weather and circumstances permitting

T.S.M.V. "LOCHFYNE"

T.S.M.V. "LOCHFYNE"

T.S.M.V. "LOCHBUIE" (Sea Coach)

M.L. "GARRY" :: :: And Other Vessels

CATERING and REFRESHMENTS on "LOCHFYNE"

AFTERNOON TEA at Points of Landing for other Vessels

DAVID MACBRAYNE LIMITED
Steam Packet Office, Fort William

The cover of the MacBraynes excursion programme from Fort William for 3-8 July 1938 featuring *Lochfyne*, *Lochbuie*, and the launch *Garry* (not illustrated). *Garry* had been built in 1937 and lasted in the fleet until 1969 serving later as a ferry at Glenelg and Rodel and finally on Loch Shiel,

MONDAY, 3rd JULY

10.15 a.m.   FORENOON CRUISE by T.S.M.V. "LOCHBUIE" (Sea Coach) to HEAD OF LOCHEIL. Magnificent view of Ben Nevis, Achdalieu, Fassifern. Due back 12.30 p.m.
Return Fare, 2/6

2.0 p.m.   CRUISE by T.S.M.V. "LOCHBUIE" (Sea Coach) to LOCH CORRIE and KINGAIRLOCH, affording magnificent views of Glencoe and Morven Mountains. 30 Minutes Ashore at Kingairloch. Due back, 6.15 p.m.   **Return Fare, 4/6**

8.15 p.m.   EVENING CRUISE by SEA COACH, "LOCHBUIE" to BALLACHULISH BAY and BONNIE LOCH LEVEN, viewing Pap of Glencoe. Due back 10.30 p.m.
Return Fare, 2/6

Also **AFTERNOON** and **EVENING CRUISES** by M.L. "GARRY."

For Regular Steamer Sailings during Week, see Brochure.

TUESDAY, 4th JULY

10.15 a.m.   FORENOON CRUISE by T.S.M.V. "LOCHBUIE" (Sea Coach) to HEAD of LOCHEIL. Magnificent view of Ben Nevis, Achdalieu, Fassifern. Due back 12.30 p.m.
Return Fare, 2/6

11.50 a.m.   To OBAN by T.S.M.V. "LOCHFYNE," viewing Castle Stalker, Lismore and Appin. Due back 8 p.m.
Return Fares :—First Class 11/-, Third Class 6/3.

2.0 p.m.   CRUISE by T.S.M.V. "LOCHBUIE" (Sea Coach) to PORT APPIN, viewing Lettermore (R. L. Stevenson's "Kidnapped"), Mountains of Morven, Castle Stalker. 30 Minutes Ashore. Due back 6.30 p.m.   **Return Fare, 4/6**

8.15 p.m.   EVENING CRUISE by T.S.M.V. "LOCHFYNE" to BONNIE LOCH LEVEN, viewing Pap of Glencoe, Ballachulish of the Slates, etc. Due back, 10.30 p.m.
Return Fare, 2/6

Also **AFTERNOON** and **EVENING CRUISES** by M.L. "GARRY."

WEDNESDAY, 5th JULY

6.40 a.m.   To STAFFA and IONA via OBAN, allowing Passengers to land on Sacred Isle, and also to Fingal's Cave at Staffa. Due back about 9 p.m.   **Return Fare, 22/6**

10.0 a.m.   LOCH SCAVAIG, by Rail to MALLAIG, thence by M.V. "LOCH NEVIS" to WEST OF SKYE. Giving time ashore for Tourists to view Loch Coruisk. Due back 8 p.m.
Return Fares :—First and Cabin, 17/3; Third and Cabin, 15/3

10.15 a.m.   FORENOON CRUISE by T.S.M.V. "LOCHBUIE" (Sea Coach) to HEAD OF LOCHEIL. Magnificent view of Ben Nevis, Achdalieu, Fassifern. Due back 12.30 p.m.
Return Fare, 2/6

2.0 p.m.   CRUISE by T.S.M.V. "LOCHBUIE" (Sea Coach) to LOCH CORRIE and KINGAIRLOCH, affording magnificent views of Glencoe and Morven Mountains. 30 Minutes ashore at Kingairloch. Due back 6.15 p.m.   **Return Fare, 4/6**

4.30 p.m.   T.S.M.V. "LOCHFYNE" EVENING CRUISE to OBAN. Returning 8.15 p.m.   **Return Fare, 2/6**

The inside pages of the Fort William excursion leaflet seen on pages 91.

Brayne's Pier, Fort William

WEDNESDAY, 5th JULY

8.15 p.m. EVENING CRUISE by T.S.M.V. "LOCHBUIE" (Sea Coach) to HEAD OF LOCHEIL. Magnificent view of Ben Nevis, Achdalieu, Fassifern. Due back 10.15 p.m.
Return Fare 2/6

Also, AFTERNOON and EVENING CRUISES by M.L. "GARRY."

THURSDAY, 6th JULY

10.15 a.m. FORENOON CRUISE by T.S.M.V. "LOCHBUIE" (Sea Coach) to HEAD OF LOCHEIL. Magnificent view of Ben Nevis, Fassifern and Achdalieu. Due back 12.30 p.m.
Return Fare, 2/6.

2.0 p.m. CRUISE by T.S.M.V. "LOCHBUIE" (Sea Coach) to PORT APPIN, viewing Lettermore (R. L. Stevenson's 'Kidnapped'), Mountains of Morven, Castle Stalker. 30 Mins. ashore. Due back 6.30 p.m.
Return Fare, 4/6

8.15 p.m. EVENING CRUISE by T.S.M.V. "LOCHBUIE" (Sea Coach) to BONNIE LOCH LEVEN, viewing Pap of Glencoe. Due back 10.30 p.m.
Return Fare, 2/6

Also, AFTERNOON and EVENING CRUISES by M.L. "GARRY."

FRIDAY, 7th JULY

10.15 a.m. FORENOON CRUISE by T.S.M.V. "LOCHBUIE" (Sea Coach) to HEAD OF LOCHEIL. Magnificent view of Ben Nevis, Fassifern and Achdalieu. Due back 12.30 p.m.
Return Fare, 2/6

2.0 p.m. CRUISE by T.S.M.V. "LOCHBUIE" (Sea Coach) to LOCH CORRIE and KINGAIRLOCH, affording magnificent views of Glencoe and Morven Mountains. 30 Minutes ashore at Kingairloch. Due back 6.15 p.m.
Return Fare, 4/6.

8.15 p.m. EVENING CRUISE by T.S.M.V. "LOCHBUIE" (Sea Coach) to HEAD OF LOCHEIL. Magnificent view of Ben Nevis, Achdalieu, Fassifern. Due back 10.15 p.m.
Return Fare 2/6

Also, AFTERNOON and EVENING CRUISES by M.L. "GARRY."

SATURDAY, 8th JULY

10.0 a.m. LOCH SCAVAIG, by Rail to MALLAIG, thence by M.V. "LOCHMHOR" to WEST OF SKYE. Giving time ashore for Tourists to view Loch Coruisk. Due back 8 p.m.
Return Fares :—First and Cabin, 17/3; Third and Cabin, 15/3.

10.15 a.m. FORENOON CRUISE by T.S.M.V. "LOCHBUIE" (Sea Coach) to HEAD OF LOCHIEL. Magnificent view of Ben Nevis, Fassifern and Achdalieu. Due back 12.30 p.m.
Return Fare 2/6

11.50 a.m. To OBAN by T.S.M.V. "LOCHFYNE", viewing Castle Stalker, Lismore and Appin. Due back 8 p.m.
Return Fares :—First Class, 11/-; Third Class, 6/3.

T.S.M.V. "LOCHBUIE" (Sea Coach, 15 knots) will be available on SATURDAY AFTERNOONS for Charter to OBAN, or any Port in the Area, or for SPECIAL CRUISE. Enquire at Office regarding Rates for your Party.

M.L. "GARRY" on SHORT CRUISES

While in Fort William

be sure to take the

FINEST ONE-DAY TOUR IN GREAT BRITAIN

by T.S.M.V. "LOCHFYNE" and
T.S.S.S. "KING GEORGE"

Each WEDNESDAY

to

FINGAL'S CAVE

(In the ISLAND OF STAFFA) and

St Columba's Sacred Isle of Iona

BURIAL PLACE OF SCOTTISH KINGS

Wednesday and Saturday

Take also that fine Excursion from MALLAIG
by T.S.M.V. "Lochnevis" to LOCH SCAVAIG
in the West of Skye. Train leaves Fort William
for Mallaig 10 a.m.

See the "Far Coolins" at their Grandest

Conditions as specified in Sailing Bills

The back page of the 1938 Fort William cruise leaflet. Cuillins is deliberately misspelt to attract attention.

Lochfyne at Tarbert. She maintained the Loch Fyne run until September 1969.

Lochfyne berthed overnight at Greenock and is seen here leaving Gourock light for Greenock during her final week in service in September 1969. She was sold the following year and, spent a spell at Faslane as a floating power station. She was later sold to Scottish & Newcastle Breweries with a view to being used as a floating pub, but nothing came of this, and in 1974 she was scrapped at Dalmuir.

In 1934 MacBraynes took over the business of Alexander Paterson of Oban and the small steamer *Princess Louise*, which had been used on short excursions form Oban. She had been built in 1898 by Ritchie, Graham & Milne at Whiteinch, and had replaced a predecessor of the same name with had been sold to the Admiralty after only four years service. The second *Princess Louise* is seen here in Oban bay with *Iona* and another unidentified steamer in the background at the North Pier.

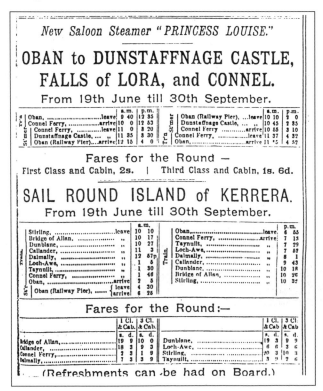

New Saloon Steamer "PRINCESS LOUISE."

OBAN to DUNSTAFFNAGE CASTLE, FALLS of LORA, and CONNEL.

From 19th June till 30th September.

	a.m.	p.m.			a.m.	p.m.
Oban, ...leave	9 40	12 35		Oban (Railway Pier), ...leave	10 10	2 0
Connel Ferry, ...arrive	10 0	12 53		Dunstaffnage Castle, ... ,,	10 45	2 35
Connel Ferry, ...leave	11 0	3 20		Connel Ferry ....arrive	10 55	3 10
Dunstaffnage Castle, ... ,,	11 35	3 30		Connel Ferry, ...leave	11 37	4 32
Oban (Railway Pier)...arrive	12 15	4 0		Oban,..........arrive	11 *5	4 52

Fares for the Round —
First Class and Cabin, 2s. | Third Class and Cabin, 1s. 6d.

SAIL ROUND ISLAND of KERRERA.

From 19th June till 30th September.

	a.m.			p.m.
Stirling, ...leave	10 10	Oban,..........leave	6 55
Bridge of Allan, ... ,,	10 17	Connel Ferry, ...arrive	7 13
Dunblane, ... ,,	10 27	Taynuilt, ... ,,	7 29
Callander, ... ,,	11 3	Loch-Awe, ... ,,	7 52
Dalmally, ... ,,	12 57p	Dalmally, ... ,,	8 1
Loch-Awe, ... ,,	1 5	Callander, ... ,,	9 43
Taynuilt, ... ,,	1 30	Dunblane, ... ,,	10 18
Connel Ferry, ... ,,	1 46	Bridge of Allan, ... ,,	10 26
Oban, ...arrive	2 5	Stirling, ... ,,	10 32
Oban (Railway Pier), ... leave	4 30		
Oban (Railway Pier), ... arrive	6 25		

Fares for the Round :—

	1 Cl. & Cab.	3 Cl. & Cab.		1 Cl. & Cab	3 Cl. & Cab
	s. d.	s. d.		s. d.	s. d.
Bridge of Allan,.........	19 9	10 0	Dunblane, ...	19 3	9 9
Callander, ...	18 3	9 3	Loch-Awe, ...	6 6	3 6
Connel Ferry,.........	2 3	1 9	Stirling, ...	20 3	10 3
Dalmally, ...	7 3	3 9	Taynuilt, ...	3 9	2 6

(Refreshments can be had on Board.)

In her early years, *Princess Louise* offered a scheduled service to Connel Ferry, as seen in this advertisement. (GEL).

A deck shot on *Princess Louise*. After purchase by MacBraynes she spent a spell at Inverness on excursion duty, and then was used on livestock sailings from Oban. She was sold in April 1939 and renamed *Bluestone*. She was destroyed by bombing whilst in dry dock at Greenock in May 1941.

A second diesel-electric ship, *Lochnevis*, joined the MacBrayne fleet in 1934. She was a smaller version of *Lochfyne*, also built by Denny of Dumbarton and is seen here on trials on the Clyde in a unique photograph. (QRC).

Lochnevis originally ran on the Mallaig to Portree mail service with a weekly sailing to Loch Scavaig and occasional cruises from Portree to Gairloch and Loch Torridon in pre-war years. During the war she served as a minelayer from December 1940 until June 1944, and was also on the Ardrishaig mail service, which was operated from Wemyss Bay at that time because of the boom between the Cloch lighthouse and Dunoon. Later she operated out of Oban and by the late sixties was offering additional weekend sailings on the West Loch Tarbert to Islay service, where she is seen here, arriving at Port Askaig.

During the sixties *Lochnevis* also saw service on the Tarbert and Ardrishaig mail run during the spell in spring which *Lochfyne* spent at Oban. She is seen here at Railway Pier, Oban, on 5 September 1969, at the berth currently used by the Mull car ferry awaiting passengers for one of her regular cruises.

Lochnevis arriving at Dunoon whilst relieving on the Tarbert and Ardrishaig mail service in the late sixties.

Lochnevis in her final season, 1969, at Gourock Pier with a Maid class vessel. She was sold to Dutch owners in 1970 and was broken up four years later, never having sailed again.

T.S. "QUEEN ALEXANDRA"

In October 1935 Williamson-Buchanan Steamers Ltd and Turbine Steamers Ltd were taken over jointly by the LMSR and Coast Lines Ltd. The latter company's two steamers *Queen Alexandra* and *King George V* were transferred to David MacBrayne Ltd, which had dropped the '(1928)' from their name the previous July. Dennys had built *Queen Alexandra* in 1912 to replace her predecessor of the same name, which had been badly damaged by fire the previous year and sold to the Canadian Pacific Railway. She is seen here on the Clyde in a postcard view in original condition.

In 1932 the promenade deck of *Queen Alexandra* had been enclosed as in this illustration. This was to bring her up to the standard of the two CSP Duchesses and *King George V* but, unlike them, there was no lounge in the newly enclosed area.

MacBraynes altered *Queen Alexandra* almost beyond recognition by adding a third (dummy) funnel to her, and, duly renamed *Saint Columba* she took the place of the revered *Columba* on the Glasgow to Ardrishaig summer service. The third funnel; was used for storing deckchairs. She is seen here in pre-war years, still with an open bridge, approaching Gourock.

After spending the war as an accommodation vessel in the East India Harbour, Greenock, *Saint Columba* did not re-appear on the Ardrishaig service until May 1947. By now this was operating from Gourock instead of Glasgow. Seen arriving at Rothesay in the Late 1940s.

THE ROYAL ROUTE

CHEAP DAY EXCURSIONS
—FROM—

ROTHESAY
—TO—

KYLES OF BUTE,

TARBERT AND ARDRISHAIG

By R.M.S. "SAINT COLUMBA"
(OR OTHER STEAMER)

1ST JUNE TILL 19TH SEPT.

GOING		RETURNING	
Rothesay, leave	10-30 a.m.	Ardrishaig, leave	1-10 p.m.
Colintraive, ,,	10-55 ,,	Tarbert, ,,	1-50 ,,
Tighnabruaich, ,,	11-10 ,,	Tighnabruaich, ,,	2-50 ,,
Tarbert, ,,	12-0 Noon	Colintraive, ,,	3-5 ,,
Ardrishaig, arrive	12-45 p.m.	Rothesay, arrive	3-40 ,,

RETURN FARES:

To COLINTRAIVE or TIGHNABRUAICH (valid day of issue only)

First Class, 2/3.   Third Class, 1/6.

To TARBERT or ARDRISHAIG (valid day of issue only, or Friday or Saturday till Tuesday).   First Class, 3/9.   Third Class, 3/-.

Tickets can be had only at MacBrayne's Office, Rothesay, or on Board Steamer

1936.   DAVID MACBRAYNE, LTD., 44 Robertson Street, Glasgow, C.2.

THE BUTEMAN, LTD, ROTHESAY

A 1936 handbill for *Saint Columba* in her first season, offering cheap day excursions from Rothesay to Tighnabruaich, Tarbert and Ardrishaig.

FROM GOUROCK AND TIGHNABRUAICH

CHEAP DAY SAILINGS

BY

R.M.S. SAINT COLUMBA

(or other Steamer)

TO

TARBERT & ARDRISHAIG

(via Kyles of Bute)
(allowing about 1¼ hours ashore at Tarbert)

(DAILY EXCEPT SUNDAYS ALL THE YEAR ROUND)

		a.m.			p.m.
GOUROCK	str. dep.	9 30	*ARDRISHAIG str. dep.		1 00
DUNOON	,, ,,	9 45	TARBERT	,, ,,	1 40
INNELLAN	,, ,,	10 00	TIGHNABRUAICH	,,	2 40
ROTHESAY	,, ,,	10 30	ROTHESAY	,, ,,	3 30
TIGHNABRUAICH	,,	11 10	INNELLAN	,, ,,	3 50
TARBERT	,, ,,	12 0n	DUNOON	,, ,,	4 10
*ARDRISHAIG	,, arr.	12 45p	GOUROCK	,, arr.	4 25

*Until 30th April and from 3rd October, Steamer terminates at Tarbert.

DAY FARES : valid day of issue only

	To Tighnabruaich (Kyles of Bute) 1st Class	To Tarbert and Ardrishaig 1st Class
From	s. d.	s. d.
GOUROCK...	7 6	10 0
TIGHNABRUAICH		6 0

TICKETS CAN BE OBTAINED FROM THE PURSER ON BOARD THE STEAMER

All passengers and their Luggage, goods and livestock, carried subject to each Company's conditions of shipment.

MEALS AND REFRESHMENTS ARE AVAILABLE ON BOARD THE STEAMER

DAVID MACBRAYNE LTD.
CLYDE HOUSE

A 1955 handbill for day return fares from Gourock to Ardrishaig.

Saint Columba arriving at Gourock, with paddle steamer *Waverley* and pilot cutter *Cantock* at the pier. (CRSC)

Saint Columba in the Kyles of Bute. In addition to the Tarbert and Ardrishaig passengers, she also carries Islay, Gigha and Jura passengers, who had travelled to West Loch Tarbert by the Islay mail steamer, thence by bus to Tarbert where they joined the *Saint Columba*.

Saint Columba and *King George V* in winter lay-up in the East India Harbour, Greenock. The former was withdrawn after the 1958 season and broken up at Port Glasgow.

ROTHESAY, ISLE OF BUTE, FROM EAST

D-3411

After her withdrawal this postcard of *Saint Columba* arriving at Rothesay was faked to make it appear she had two funnels, the publishers apparently hoping that she would be mistaken for the *Duchess of Hamilton* or *Montrose*. At the pier are a *Maid* and an ABC car ferry.

T.S. "KING GEORGE V." ON CRUISE ROUND AILSA CRAIG.   203331.

The other turbine steamer to join MacBraynes in 1936 was *King George* V. Built in 1926, she had been initially fitted with experimental high-pressure turbine machinery. She is seen here in her original condition in 1926 in a postcard view off Dunoon with the Cloch lighthouse in the background, although the caption states 'T.S. *King George* V on cruise round Ailsa Craig', a cruise she never undertook.

King George V entered service for David MacBrayne Ltd in 1936 on the route she was to make her own for almost the next forty years, from Oban to Staffa and Iona. She was altered to have six lifeboats instead of the previous four, the extra two having been carried previously on *Columba* and before that, *Scout*. She is seen here in Rothsay bay in 1936.

106

Pleasure Sailings
FROM
North Pier, Oban

T.T.S.S. "KING GEORGE V."

BY SALOON STEAMERS

T.T.S.S. "KING GEORGE V."

T.S.V. "LOCHFYNE"

P.S. "MOUNTAINEER"

(Weather, etc., permitting)

BREAKFAST——LUNCHEON——TEA

AND OTHER REFRESHMENTS MAY BE HAD ON BOARD

DAVID MACBRAYNE LTD.
Steam Packet Office
NORTH PIER, OBAN

The cover of the Oban Excursion programme for 1936. (GEL).

MONDAY, 3rd AUGUST

6.0 a.m. To INNER HEBRIDES (Tobermory, Coll, Tiree, Castlebay and Lochboisdale) by magnificent NEW MOTOR VESSEL, "LOCHEARN." One night on board. Due back Tuesday afternoon.

9.5 a.m. To STAFFA AND IONA and round MULL, calling TOBERMORY 4-5 p.m. due back about 6—5 p.m.

11.50 a.m. To BALLACHULISH (Kentallen Pier) for GLENCOE, due back 6.40 p.m.

11.50 a.m. To FORT WILLIAM, due back 6.40 p.m.

2.30 p.m. "MOUNTAINEER" CRUISE to ISLES OF THE SEA (Holy Isles), St. Columba's Landing Place, by Sound of Kerrera, passing Kilbowie and Gallanach, Gylen Castle, Easdale and Luing, and affording magnificent views of Mull, Jura, and Lorn Mountains. Returning to Oban about 5.15 p.m. **Return Fare, 2/6**

6.45 p.m. EVENING CRUISE to LISMORE by Steamer "MOUNTAINEER." Due back 8.20 p.m. **Return Fare, 1/6**

TUESDAY, 4th AUGUST

8.45 a.m. To BALLACHULISH (Kentallen Pier) for GLENCOE, due back 2.15 p.m.

8.45 a.m. To FORT WILLIAM, due back 2.15 p.m.

9.5 a.m. To STAFFA AND IONA, calling TOBERMORY 10.35 a.m., and round MULL. Due back about 6.5 p.m.

9.5 a.m. To TOBERMORY, by Turbine Vessel "KING GEORGE V." and returning by M.V. "LOCHEARN" from Tobermory, 12 noon. Passengers have about one hour ashore. **Special Day Return, 5/-**

10.30 a.m. Excursion to TOBERMORY and LOCH SUNART, by P.S. "MOUNTAINEER," due back about 6 p.m. After leaving Tobermory for Loch Sunart the Steamer strikes across Auliston Point and ascends the winding reaches of Loch Sunart, past Oronsay Island on the right, and Glenborrodale Castle on the left. Steamer leaves Tobermory on the return journey at 3.30 p.m., passing Dunollie and Duart Castles, Lady Rock, Torosay and Ardtornish Castles. **Special Return Fare, 6/-**

2.30 p.m. To LOCH CRERAN, by T.S.V. "LOCHFYNE," due back about 5 p.m. Passing Dunollie and Dunstaffnage Castles, viewing Connel Bridge and Beregonium Eriska Island, Lismore, and up Loch Creran, viewing Barcaldine Castle, and grand scenery on the North side of Loch Creran and Creagan Narrows. **Return Fare, 2/6**

6.0 p.m. To FORT WILLIAM and Intermediate Ports, returning following morning at 6.40 a.m.

WEDNESDAY, 5th AUGUST

6.0 a.m. To INNER HEBRIDES (Tobermory, Coll, Tiree, Castlebay and Lochboisdale) by magnificent NEW MOTOR VESSEL "LOCHEARN." One night on board. Due back Thursday afternoon.

9.5 a.m. To STAFFA AND IONA and round MULL, calling TOBERMORY 4-5 p.m. due back about 6—5 p.m.

10.30 a.m. EXCURSION to CRINAN, by P.S. "MOUNTAINEER," allowing passengers about one hour ashore at Crinan. Due back 5 p.m. Steamer passes through Sound of Kerrera, viewing Kilbowie and Gallanach, Gylen Castle, Easdale and Luing; also Loch Melfort, with its archipelago of small isles at the entrance. An excellent view is offered of the Mull, Jura and Lorn Mountains. **Special Return Fare, 6/-**

11.50 a.m. To BALLACHULISH (Kentallen Pier) for GLENCOE, due back 6.40 p.m.

11.50 a.m. To FORT WILLIAM, due back 6.40 p.m.

6.40 p.m. GRAND EVENING CRUISE To FORT WILLIAM, by T.S.V. "LOCHFYNE." Due back 11 p.m. **Return Fare, 2/6**

6.45 p.m. EVENING CRUISE to LISMORE by Steamer "MOUNTAINEER." Due back 8.20 p.m. **Return Fare, 1/6**

FARES—

FOR INNER HEBRIDES TOUR (including berth, one night), First Class, 40/-; Third Class, 26/- Cabin passengers may embark on evening prior to day of sailing at a charge of 3/- per berth.
Children above 3 and under 14 years are charged half fare.

The centre pages of the above programme, showing sailings from 3-8 August by *King George V*,

THURSDAY, 6th AUGUST

8.45 a.m. To BALLACHULISH (Kentallen Pier) for GLENCOE, due back 2.15 p.m.

8.45 a.m. To FORT WILLIAM, due back 2.15 p.m.

9.5 a.m. To STAFFA AND IONA, calling TOBERMORY 10.35 a.m., and round MULL. Due back about 6.5 p.m.

9.5 a.m. To TOBERMORY, by Turbine Vessel "KING GEORGE V." and returning by M.V. "LOCHEARN" from Tobermory, 12 noon. Passengers have about one hour ashore. **Special Day Return, 5/-**

10.30 a.m. EXCURSION to LOCHSPELVE and SALEN, MULL, by P.S. "Mountaineer." Allowing passengers about one hour ashore at Salen. Due back about 5 p.m. Steamer passes through Sound of Kerrera, viewing Kilbowie and Gallanach, Gylen Castle, Loch Spelve, Lochdon, Duart Castle, Ardtornish Castle. **Special Return Fare, 6/-**

2.30 p.m. To LOCH CRERAN, by T.S.V. "LOCHFYNE," due back about 5 p.m. Passing Dunollie and Dunstaffnage Castles, viewing Connel Bridge and Beregonium, Eriska Island, Lismore, and up Loch Creran, viewing Barcaldine Castle, and grand scenery on the North side of Loch Creran and Creagan Narrows. **Return Fare, 2/6**

6.15 p.m. GRAND EVENING CRUISE to TOBERMORY, by T.S.V. "LOCHFYNE." Due back 9.30 p.m. **Return Fare, 2/6**

FRIDAY, 7th AUGUST

6.0 a.m. To INNER HEBRIDES (Tobermory, Coll, Tiree, Castlebay and Lochboisdale) by magnificent NEW MOTOR VESSEL, "LOCHEARN." One night on board. Due back Saturday afternoon.

9.5 a.m. To STAFFA AND IONA and round MULL, calling TOBERMORY 4-5 p.m. due back about 6—5 p.m.

10.30 a.m. **MORVERN HIGHLAND GAMES**

"MOUNTAINEER" calling at Craignure and Lochaline. Returning from Lochaline at 4.30 p.m. for Craignure and Oban. Oban arrive 6 p.m. DAY RETURN FARES will be issued.

10.30 a.m. Excursion to TOBERMORY and LOCH SUNART, by P.S. "MOUNTAINEER," due back about 6 p.m. Steamer leaves Tobermory on the return journey at 3.30 p.m. passing Dunollie and Duart Castles, Lady Rock, Torosay and Ardtornish Castles. After leaving Tobermory the Steamer strikes across Auliston Point and ascends the winding reaches of Loch Sunart, past Oronsay Island on the right, and Glenborrodale Castle on the left. **Special Return Fare, 6/-**

11.50 a.m. To BALLACHULISH (Kentallen Pier) for GLENCOE, due back 6.40 p.m.

11.50 a.m. To FORT WILLIAM, due back 6.40 p.m.

6.45 p.m. EVENING CRUISE to LISMORE by Steamer "MOUNTAINEER." Due back 8.20 p.m. **Return Fare, 1/6**

SATURDAY, 8th AUGUST

8.45 a.m. To BALLACHULISH (Kentallen Pier) for GLENCOE, due back 2.15 p.m.

8.45 a.m. To FORT WILLIAM, due back 2.15 p.m.

9.5 a.m. To STAFFA AND IONA, calling TOBERMORY 10.35 a.m., and round MULL. Due back about 6.5 p.m.

9.5 a.m. To TOBERMORY, by Turbine Vessel "KING GEORGE V." and returning by M.V. "LOCHEARN" from Tobermory, 12 noon. **Special Day Return, 5/-**

2.30 p.m. CRUISE TO LOCH CORRY, by T.S.V. "LOCHFYNE," due back Oban about 5 p.m. Passing Dunollie and Dunstaffnage Castles, viewing Connel Bridge and Beregonium, Eriska Island, Lismore, etc., etc. **Return Fare, 2/6**

6.0 p.m. To FORT WILLIAM and Intermediate Ports, returning following morning at

SPECIAL NOTICE—TOBERMORY REGATTA

9.5 a.m. "KING GEORGE V." to TOBERMORY. Returning at 8 p.m. direct to Oban. The Glasgow Corporation Gas Department Prize Brass Band will play on board on the passage.

10 a.m. "MOUNTAINEER" Special Trip to TOBERMORY, calling at Craignure, Lochaline, Salen, and Drimnin. Return journey from Tobermory at 4.30 p.m. for Oban and intermediate ports.

DAY RETURN FARES will be issued from all ports of call.

6.15 p.m. GRAND EVENING CRUISE to TOBERMORY by "KING GEORGE V." Due back about 9.45 p.m. The Glasgow Corporation Gas Department Prize Brass Band will play on the passage from Tobermory to Oban. **Special Return Fare, 2/6**

DAY RETURN FARES:—

To STAFFA AND IONA, including Boatmen and Guides, ... **20/-**
        or including luncheon and plain tea, ... **24/9**
To BALLACHULISH (Kentallen Pier), ... First Class, 7/6; Third Class, 4/6
To BALLACHULISH (Kentallen Pier) including Glencoe Drive, ... First, 11/6; Third, 8/6
To FORT WILLIAM, ... First Class, 10/6; Third Class, 6/-
Children above 3 and under 14 years are charged half fare.

Lochfyne and *Mountaineer*. (GEL).

WHILE IN OBAN

DO NOT FAIL TO DO THIS TOUR

The Finest One-Day Tour in Great Britain

By T.T.S.S. "KING GEORGE V." (or other Steamer)

TO

FINGAL'S CAVE

(In the ISLAND OF STAFFA) and

ST. COLUMBA'S

SACRED ISLE OF IONA

Burial Place of Scottish Kings

POPULAR EXCURSION FROM

OBAN to INVERNESS and back

Via FORT WILLIAM and CALEDONIAN CANAL

RETURN FARES: 1st Class, 40/-; 3rd Class, 21/-

TICKETS VALID TO BREAK JOURNEY AND TO
RETURN WITHIN SIX DAYS FROM DATE OF ISSUE

Steamer leaves Oban on Tuesdays, Thursdays and Saturdays at **8.45** a.m. and due Inverness **6.40** p.m. For the return journey to Oban the Steamer leaves Inverness on Mondays, Wednesdays and Fridays at **8.30** a.m., and the passengers are due in Oban at **6.40** p.m. same day.

A sail up the world-famous Caledonian Canal is a never-to-be-forgotten experience. Some sixty miles in length, forty of which are natural lochs, studded here and there with islet gems, the beauty of which fascinates and charms, while the rugged pine-clad hills enfold one in a moving panorama impossible to describe. The district, too, is steeped in the romance and lore of Lochiel and Lovat, Chiefs of the ancient clans of Cameron and Fraser—a wonderful country, beautiful and awe-inspiring in its grandeur—the Caledonian Canal must be seen to be appreciated. No pen can do it justice.

The Inner Hebrides Tour

THE OPPORTUNE TIME TO VISIT THE INNER ISLANDS IS NOW.
Travel the Comfort way by the magnificent new Motor Vessel " Lochearn,"
making the Steamer your Hotel for two days

The Owners reserve the right to alter or cancel any of these trips as may be found necessary.

All Passengers and their Luggage and Goods and Live Stock are only carried subject to the conditions specified on back of the Company's General Sailing Bills.

Illustrated Brochure and Time Table free, can be had on application to Steamer Office, North Pier, Oban.

Tickets can be had on board or from

DAVID MACBRAYNE LTD.

STEAM PACKET OFFICE,

OBAN.

OBAN TIMES LIMITED.

The rear page of the 1936 Oban excursion programme.

King George V in pre-war days with Kerrera and the Hutcheson monument behind.

STEAMER ARRIVING AT RAILWAY PIER, OBAN.

King George V arriving at the Railway Pier at Oban with the *Lochfyne* in the background. A postcard view from 1947 as in the following year she was fitted with a wheelhouse.

THE PIER FROM THE STATION, FORT WILLIAM

King George V at Fort William in 1948 or 1949. Her external doors were painted white in 1950. She offered an Iona sailing in most seasons once a week from Fort William, generally sailing south of Mull from Oban in both directions, although in certain years the Oban call was omitted and she sailed directly from Fort William to Tobermory, and directly back from Iona. In her final years from 1970 onwards when she was the sole Oban excursion steamer, she offered Fort William sailings from Oban on certain days, as well as a Tobermory and Loch Sunart Cruise, and a Six Lochs cruise.

A post-1952 view of Oban from Pulpit Hill with *King George V* berthed at the Railway Pier. As well as a wheelhouse, she had in that year been fitted with a mainmast. *Lochness* can just be seen berthed aft of her.

King George V saw occasional service in the Clyde, as in this illustration of her arriving at Glasgow Bridge Wharf on 2 June 1956 on a charter to the Kyles of Bute. Whilst on this cruise she met up with *Saint Columba* at Rothesay, the only occasion when these two steamers shared a pier whilst in MacBrayne ownership.

King George V saw war service as a tender on the Clyde and also as a troop transport, after being present at the Dunkirk evacuation. In 1946 she maintained the summer Ardrishaig service as *Saint Columba* had not yet been released from war service, and from 1947 was back on the round Mull run. Seen here passing Corran Ferry.

The bell and builders plate of 'King George V, *built by Wm. Denny & Bros Ltd, Dumbarton, 1926, engined by The Parsons Marine Steam Turbine Co. Ltd. Newcastle-upon-Tyne'.*

King George V moving across Oban Bay towards the Railway Pier in the sixties. In 1960 the after lifeboats had been replaced by inflatable life rafts.

King George V refulling at her overnight berth at the Railway Pier. She would normally move across the bay from here to the North Pier to take on passengers each morning. A shot taken on 14 September 1970.

King George V at Tobermory, probably in 1972, with the Mingary vessel *Lochnell* just visible in the foreground. On occasions when bad weather precluded her sailing in the open sea to Staffa and on to Iona, she would offer an extended call at Tobermory, before returning to Oban.

King George V off Staffa in a faked postcard. Passengers were landed at Staffa for a visit to Fingal's Cave until the path was blocked by a rock fall in 1964. A landing at Staffa was often not possible because the seas were too rough for the 'wee red boats' which acted as tenders to come over from Iona.

King George V at anchor off Iona on 5 September 1969 with *Ulva*, one of the motor boats which acted as tenders there, just forward of her.

King George V in winter lay up in early 1968 in Queens Dock, Glasgow.

King George V crossing to the North Pier at Oban in her 1973 Caledonian MacBrayne colours. In 1974 her ventilators were painted grey and at the end of that season she was withdrawn.

King George V was withdrawn after the close of the 1974 season. She was sold and towed to dry dock in Cardiff in April 1975. She lay there for a number of years, the subject of various abortive plans to open her as a restaurant or pub, until seriously damaged by fire in August 1981, after which she was beached in the River Taff and allowed to break up naturally. A sad end for a fine ship. She is seen here in early 1978.

Lochgorm, seen here in Kingston Dock. To the left was another inter-company transfer by Coast Lines. She had previously been Burns & Laird Lines' *Lairdspool*, and had been built in 1896 by Blackwood and Gordon of Port Glasgow, as Laird Line's *Lily*. She served MacBraynes on the Glasgow to Stornoway cargo route from 1937 until sold in 1951 for scrapping at Port Glasgow. The small steamer in the right foreground is *Marie* of 1904, owned by Clyde & Campbeltown Shipping Co. Ltd. (QRC).

Lochgarry, purchased by MacBraynes in 1937, also came from Burns & Laird having been their *Lairdsrock*, originally Burns *Vulture*, built in 1898 by A.&J. Inglis. She replaced the *Lochbroom* on the Glasgow to West Highlands passenger service. She was requisitioned for war service in 1940, served at Dunkirk and was lost during a gale on 21 January 1942 off Rathlin while being used as a transport between the Clyde and Iceland. (QRC).

The first *Lochbuie* was described as a sea-coach when built, being fitted with bus-type seating and intended to be similar to the sea-buses and fjord-buses in operation in Norway. Originally intended to run from Oban to Craignure in connection with a bus operator on Mull, that plan had to be abandoned after the bus operation went out of business, and she entered service on short trips from Fort William, where she is seen here. She was built in Amsterdam in 1937 with Man diesel engines. In September 1939 she was requisitioned and served as a naval hospital launch on the Clyde named *Roundalay*. She was sold in 1947 to British Channel Islands Shipping Co., a Coast Lines company, and was registered at Poole as *Silver Coast*. Although some sources state that she ran local excursion from there, this has not been confirmed. In 1950 she was converted to the yacht *Marlene*. (GEL).

Lochiel was a quasi-sister ship of *Lochnevis*, built by Denny of Dumbarton in 1939 for the Islay service. Seen here in trials, she spent part of the 1939 season at Oban, on the Fort William service, prior to the pier at West Loch Tarbert being extended for her. She served as the Portree mail steamer in the 1939-1940 winter and made occasional runs to Oban with livestock etc, but remained almost exclusively on the Islay service until withdrawn in January 1970. (QRC).

THE MAIL STEAMER AT PORT ASKAIG, ISLAY.   A.9755.

Lochiel at Port Askaig prior to 1953 when she was fitted with a mainmast.

After withdrawal *Lochiel* operated for the 1970 summer as *Norwest Laird* from Fleetwood to Douglas for Norwest Hovercraft. She is seen here at Douglas inner harbour.

Lochiel then served for many years at Bristol as a floating pub/restaurant for Courage Breweries until scrapped in 1995

MacBraynes chartered *Robina* in 1946 and 1947. She had been built in 1914 to operate out of Morecambe on excursion sailings. In 1920 she served on the Bristol Channel, and was sold in 1925 to Belfast owners. In January 1946 she was purchased by Coast Lines Ltd and was chartered to David MacBrayne Ltd from June of that year. In 1946 she ran excursions from Oban, similar to those which had been operated by the *Princess Louise*, and in 1947 was on the Gourock to Lochgoilhead mail service in succession to Comet. She is seen here in Loch Goil taken from PS *Waverley*, which was then in her first season. In 1948 she was chartered to a Coast Lines subsidiary in Guernsey and was sold to the Southampton, Isle of Wight, & South of England RMSP in August of that year. She was scrapped in 1953 in Holland. (GEL).

MacBraynes first new building after the war was the *Loch Seaforth*, delivered from Denny in 1947. She served on the Mallaig and Kyle to Stornoway mail service in succession to the *Lochness* and is seen here leaving Mallaig.

Loch Seaforth boasted a bow crest of a Highlander, by this time the MacBrayne motif, seen to its advantage her in a view of her at Mallaig in summer 1968.

Loch Seaforth leaving Mallaig in a postcard view.

Loch Seaforth at Mallaig in a view taken in 1967.

Loch Seaforth at Stornoway, in what appears to be a faked postcard, with the funnel of *Loch Dunvegan* just visible to the left. She served the Stornoway run until 1972, when she transferred to the Inner Islands service from Oban to Coll, Tiree, Castlebay and Lochboisdale. On 22 March 1973 she ran aground on Cleit Rock in the sound of Gunna and, after being freed, was towed to Tiree, where she sank at the pier. She was not refloated until early May and was then towed to Troon for scrapping.

Lismore, previously served by the Sound of Mull service, got its own service from 1947. The *Lochnell* was purchased for this service. She had previously been the hospital launch *Galen*, built in 1941 by Silver of Rosneath. From 1965 she carried out the Kyle to Toscaig run and from 1968 that from Tobermory to Mingary. She is seen here at Kyle. She was sold in 1981 and saw a spell of service on the Clyde, operating out of Renfrew.

In 1990 *Lochnell* operated as *Loch Nell* on Loch Leven cruises from a jetty at Ballachulish. At the time of writing she has been laid up in the River Cart at Paisley now for a few years following a sinking and fire at Ballachulish.

Passengers booked through by Carron Company's Steamers.

GLASGOW AND THE HIGHLANDS.

STEAMER

"DUNARA
CASTLE."
453 Tons.

WEEKLY CIRCULAR TOUR

BY THE FAVOURITE STEAMER

"DUNARA CASTLE,"

From GLASGOW, every Thursday, at 2 p.m., and
from GREENOCK, at 7 p.m., for

COLONSAY, IONA, MULL, TYREE, SKYE, HARRIS, UIST, and BARRA.

Returning to GLASGOW on Wednesday morning.

The scenery is most varied, and is unequalled for solitary grandeur, and wild and savage magnificence. It teems with incidents romantic and tragic which have been rendered famous by the pens of the historian, the poet, and the novelist. Glimpses are to be had of the primitive ways of life that are fast becoming obsolete.

Cabin Fare for the Round, - - - £1 15s.
Do.   do.   (including Meals), £3 5s.

Occasional Special Trips to the Island of St. Kilda.
Return Cabin Fare, including Meals, £4 4s.

Time Bills, with Maps, and Berths secured, on application to
MARTIN ORME, 20 Robertson Street, GLASGOW.

A 1895 Martin Orme advert for cruises in the *Dunara Castle*, showing her in two-funnelled condition, although she had been altered to a single funnel when re-boilered the previous year. (GEL).

Five
Semi-Nationalised
1948-1972

S. S. "Hebrides" at Portaskaig

On 1 January 1948 not only were MacBraynes 50% nationalised with the formation of British Railways, but they also took over their only competitor in the West Highland trade, McCallum, Orme & Co. Ltd. That company had been formed in 1929 by the merger of the McCallum and Orme fleets, and had absorbed the firm of Jack Bros in 1935. *Hebrides* had been built in 1898 by Ailsa of Troon for McCallum and operated from Glasgow to the islands with cargo and round-trip passengers, with occasional visits to the outpost of St Kilda. She is seen here at Port Askaig on Islay.

S.S. Hebrides, at Pooltiel Pier, Glendale.

Hebrides at Pooltiel Pier, Glendale on Skye. After being taken over by MacBraynes she continued in the Outer Islands cargo service from Glasgow until sold for scrapping at Port Glasgow in 1955.

The second steamer taken over with McCallum Orme was the *Dunara Castle*. She had been built in 1875 for Martin Orme, and had had a similar career to *Hebrides*. She had taken part in the evacuation of the last permanent inhabitants of St Kilda in 1930. Notable in this illustration is the McCallum, Orme house flag flying from the mainmast.

GLASGOW

AND THE

WEST HIGHLANDS

THE UNDERNOTED OR OTHER STEAMERS ARE INTENDED TO SAIL WITH GOODS AND PASSENGERS

As under (until further notice, and unless prevented by any unforeseen circumstances)

FROM
GLASGOW
Berth 44
Lancefield Quay
AT
2.30 P.M.

FROM
GREENOCK
AT
6.30 P.M.

"HEBRIDES"

Calling at Custom House Quay, Greenock

ON	TO
THURSDAY, 10th MAY	Portaskaig
	Colonsay
	Oban
	Tobermory
MONDAY, 21st MAY Including CRUISE ROUND ISLE OF SKYE	Coll
	Tiree
	Barra {Castlebay / Northbay}
THURSDAY, 31st MAY Including CALL AT ST. KILDA	Lochboisdale
	Skipport
	Carnan
	Scotvin (Kallin)
MONDAY, 11th JUNE Including CRUISE ROUND ISLE OF SKYE	Loch Eport
	Lochmaddy
	Tarbert (Harris)
	Uig
THURSDAY, 21st JUNE Including CALL AT ST. KILDA	Dunvegan
	Colbost
	Pooltiel
	*Struan
	Carbost
MONDAY, 2nd JULY Including CRUISE ROUND ISLE OF SKYE	Coll
	Tiree
	Tobermory
	Oban
	Colonsay
	Portaskaig

* NOTE—No call at STRUAN on Sailings of 10th May, 31st May and 21st June

"DUNARA CASTLE"

Calling at West Quay, Greenock

ON	TO
THURSDAY, 3rd MAY	Colonsay
	Iona
	Bunessan
	Tiree
	Elgoll
MONDAY, 14th MAY	Soay
	Portnalong
	Carbost
	Struan
	Pooltiel
THURSDAY, 24th MAY Including CALL AT LOCH SCAVAIG	Colbost
	Dunvegan
	Stein
	Uig
MONDAY, 4th JUNE Including CALL AT LOCH ROAG	Tarbert (Harris)
	Scalpay
	Finsbay
	Leverburgh
	Lochmaddy
THURSDAY, 14th JUNE Including CALL AT ST. KILDA	Kallin (Scotvin)
	Carnan
	Lochboisdale
	Barra {Castlebay / Northbay}
MONDAY, 25th JUNE Including CALL AT LOCH SCAVAIG	Tiree
	Bunessan
	Iona
	Colonsay

AND ANY OTHER PORTS THAT MAY BE AGREED UPON.

"Hebrides" leaves OBAN going North the following day after Glasgow Sailing Date, NOT BEFORE 1 P.M. [redacted] and leaves Oban again when coming South not before 1 p.m. on 5th, 16th and 28th May, and 7th, 18th and 28th June respectively

FARES FROM GLASGOW OR GREENOCK

	† Cabin.	Steerage.
PORTASKAIG, ISLAY,	17/3	10/3
COLONSAY,	20/-	10/6
IONA and BUNESSAN	25/-	10/6
COLL and TIREE,	25/-	12/6
BARRA,	34/3	15/-
HARRIS,	60/-	15/-

†Sleeping Berth 2s. 6d. extra.

*CRUISES, Board included— { St. Kilda, Loch Roag, Loch Scavaig & Round Skye } Cabin Return. £10 0/-

*Berths in Four-Berthed Rooms, 2s. 6d. extra; in Two-Berthed Rooms and Deck Cabins, 5s. extra.

CRUISE SAILING DATES.

ST. KILDA—31st May, 14th and 21st June, 12th and 16th July, 2nd and 16th August.
LOCH ROAG, LEWIS—4th June, 5th July, 6th August and 6th September.
LOCH SCAVAIG for LOCH CORUISK, SKYE—24th May, 25th June, 26th July, 23rd and 27th August, 13th and 17th September.
ROUND THE ISLE OF SKYE—21st May, 11th June, 2nd and 23rd July, 13th August and 3rd September.

☛ All FREIGHTS must be PREPAID, except for PORTASKAIG, OBAN and TOBERMORY, and senders by Railway or Carrier must instruct the latter to pay through.

For further particulars, apply in Portaskaig to A. CURRIE & CO.; in Oban to DUNCAN MACDOUGALL, Railway Pier and Albany Street, Telephone, Oban 54; in Tobermory to JOHN M'FARLANE; in Greenock to JAS. S. MILLAR, Customhouse Quay, Telephone, Greenock 686; or to—

NOTE.—All Passengers and their Luggage, Goods and Live Stock are only carried subject to the conditions specified on back hereof. Such conditions are held to include that delivery is completed at the Ship's side without signature, whether Goods or Live Stock are discharged at Pier or into Ferryboat. Goods and Live Stock are only carried at their Owner's risk, and all contingencies should be insured against. Special warning of the conditions under which Goods are Shipped is hereby given to Shippers of Glass, Crockery, Furniture, Cast Iron, Rain Water Goods, Live Stock, Sugar, and all Goods liable to damage by rain, sea, or other water or damp. Goods are only accepted and signed for subject to the Conditions of Shipment, Inward Condition, weight and contents unknown.

IMPORTANT NOTICE.

SHIPPERS, RAILWAY and OTHER CARRIERS are respectfully informed :—

Every article offered for shipment must bear a label shewing distinctly Consignee's name and the landing place. Postal addresses frequently give no indication of the correct landing place, and should be avoided, unless of course in cases where the postal address and the landing place are one and the same.

Sailings are subject to alteration without notice, and Owners are not responsible for any delays to Passengers or Goods that may arise through Strikes, Lockouts or any other cause whatever

McCallum, Orme sailing bill for *Hebrides* and *Dunara Castle* for May and June 1934. Note the cruise sailing dates at the bottom for special sailings to St. Kilda, Loch Roag on Lewis, Loch Scavaig and Round the Isle of Skye. (GEL).

Dunara Castle on the Clyde at Lancefield Quay with the Finnieston vehicular ferry and *Hebrides* astern of the ferry berth. *Dunara Castle* only operated for one month for MacBraynes and was broken up at Port Glasgow in summer 1948.

The third steamer taken over with McCallum Orme was the *Challenger*, which had come from the Jack Bros. fleet. She had been built in 1897 by Hall Russell at Aberdeen and came under the ownership of James Jack in 1929. She is seen here passing Dalmuir and served only a few months in the MacBrayne fleet, being sold for scrap in November 1948. Note that her wheelhouse was not equipped with glazed windows. (GEL).

MACBRAYNES STEAMERS

Incorporating the Services of McCALLUM ORME & Co., Ltd.

CARGO SAILINGS

FROM

GLASGOW &

GREENOCK

JANUARY, 1948 (Weather and circumstances permitting).

BY THE FOLLOWING OR OTHER STEAMERS.

M.V. "LOCHSHIEL"

LOADING BERTH - 4 KINGSTON DOCK   2nd, 12th and 22nd JANUARY

To Port Ellen, Gigha, Luing, Oban, Lismore, Kingairloch, Kinlochleven, Fort William, Tobermory, Mingarry, Glenborrodale, Glencirspesdale, Laudale, Strontian, Salen-Loch Sunart. On 22nd Calls also Ardlussa, Croggan, Calgary, Ulva, Gometra, Tavool, Tiroran.

S.S. "LOCHDUNVEGAN"

LOADING BERTH - 4 KINGSTON DOCK   7th, 14th, 21st and 28th JANUARY

To Islay and Jura. To Gigha (via Port Ellen).

S.S. "ULSTER STAR"

LOADING BERTH - 6 KINGSTON DOCK   6th, 13th, 20th and 27th JANUARY

To Tobermory, Drimnin, Kilchoan, Portree, Raasay, and Stornoway.

S.S. "LOCHGORM"

LOADING BERTH - 6 KINGSTON DOCK   8th, 19th and 29th JANUARY

To Oban, Craignure, Lochaline, Salen, (Mull), Tobermory, Drimnin, Kilchoan, Eigg, Mallaig, Armadale, Glenelg, Kyle of Lochalsh, Raasay, Portree, Gairloch, Aultbea, Scorraig, Ullapool, Baden-Tarbet, Lochinver, Stockinish, Rodel, Canna, Rhum. On 29th calls also at Lochinchard, (Lochclash Pier).

S.S. "HEBRIDES"

LOADING BERTH - 46 LANCEFIELD QUAY   12th and 21st JANUARY

To Colonsay, Oban, Barra, Lochboisdale, Skipport, Kallin, Locheport, Lochmaddy, Tarbert, Uig, Dunvegan, Pooltiel, Portnalong, Carbost, Tobermory, Oban, Colonsay.

S.S. "CHALLENGER"

LOADING BERTH - 46 LANCEFIELD QUAY   7th, 19th and 28th JANUARY

To Colonsay, Elgoll and Soay, Dunvegan, Uig, Scalpay, Tarbert, Finsbay, Leverburgh, Lochmaddy, Kallin, Skipport, Lochboisdale, Eriskay, Barra, Colonsay, No call at Greenock

S.S. "DUNARA CASTLE"

LOADING BERTH - 46 LANCEFIELD QUAY   2nd, 8th, 15th, 22nd and 29th JANUARY

To Port Askaig, Colonsay, Oban, Tobermory, Coll, Tiree, Bunessan, Iona, Oban, Colonsay, Port Askaig.

The order in which the Calls may be made is entirely at the discretion of the Masters of the Steamers, who will be guided by circumstances. Shippers should arrange with the undersigned as to Shipments, before actually sending down the Goods to the Sheds.

GOODS FOR STRUAN, COLBOST AND STEIN (WATERNISH) ARE ACCEPTED TO LAND AT DUNVEGAN, AND FOR CARNAN AND PETERSPORT TO LAND AT SKIPPORT, THENCE PER MOTOR TRANSPORT, BUT SHOULD BE DISTINCTLY ADDRESSED TO THEIR FINAL DESTINATION.

**44 ROBERTSON STREET,
GLASGOW, C.2., DEC., 1947.**

DAVID MACBRAYNE, LTD.
TEL: CENTRAL 9954/59.

ARCHIBALD SINCLAIR, 2-12 MACKEITH STREET, GLASGOW, S.E.

MacBrayne cargo sailing bill for January 1948 showing the last sailings of the *Dunara Castle*. *Ulster Star* was a chartered steamer. She had been built in 1904 and was on charter, replacing the *Lochgarry*, from 1942 until sold for scrapping in February 1949.

The ten years following the Second World War saw a series of cargo vessels built and purchased, thus replacing a number of veterans in the fleet. *Lochbroom* was the first of these. Scott of Bowling had built her in 1945 as the steamer *Empire Maysong*. On purchase by MacBraynes in December 1948, a diesel engine replaced the steam machinery and she entered service on the cargo run from Glasgow to Islay and Portree. She served latterly as a spare cargo vessel, and was sold in July 1971 to Cypriot owners and was renamed *Focomar*. She ran aground on the coast of Andros and sank in September 1974. She is seen here in lay up at Greenock's James Watt Dock in January 1970 with *Lochnevis* behind her. Note that her bow had been cut 12 inches to avoid a mainmast having to be fitted.

The second *Lochbuie* was purchased in 1949 to operate from Tobermory to Mingary, a port that had previously been served by the Outer Islands mail steamer from Oban. She had been built at East Cowes in 1942 as an RAF fast rescue launch and was rebuilt and re-engined before entering service. She is seen here in a photo taken from the *Lochearn* with the Coast Lines cruise ship *Lady Killarney* behind her. She served the route until broken up in 1968. (GEL).

The second new cargo vessel was *Loch Frisa*. She had been built in Canada in 1948 to a standard wartime design as the *Marleen*. She had been under Dutch ownership when purchased and served on the cargo routes from Glasgow until sold in 1963 to Greek owners and was scrapped by the early eighties. She was the last steamer to be purchased by MacBraynes and is seen here in lay up in the East India Harbour at Greenock, alongside *Lochinvar*.

Lochdunvegan was en ex-Swedish cargo vessel. She had been built at Gothenburg in 1946 and named *Örnen*. Purchased by MacBraynes in 1950 she replaced the *Lochgorm* on the Glasgow to Stornoway cargo service. She is seen here sailing up the Clyde passing Harland & Wolff's yard at Govan. (QRC).

In summer 1973 *Lochdunvegan* was employed as a car ferry from Oban to Tiree, and is seen here off Oban on 28 July 1973. She was withdrawn in November of that year following a grounding and was also sold to Greek owners, sailing under the names *Fanis*, *Vassilis* and *Maggy* respectively.

Loch Carron was the first of the new cargo vessels to be built for the company. She was built by the Ardrossan Dockyard Ltd, and was launched in 1951. She served to Outer Islands cargo run from Glasgow, and is seen here in Kingston Dock on the day of her entering service in 1951, with the bow of the *Taransay*, which at that time was operating from Glasgow to Campbeltown, just visible to the left

Loch Carron in the sound of Mull. Note the car carried as deck cargo. (QRC).

Loch Carron at the Bristol Berth at Greenock in August 1975. Note the *Claymore* and *Maid of Cumbrae* just visible inside the East India Harbour. By 1976 she had become the last coastal cargo vessel to operate from Glasgow. In 1977 she was sold to Cypriot owners and was reported to have sank in the 1980s.

Lochshiel was built in 1953 for service on Loch Shiel and was originally named *Rosalind*. At that time MacBraynes recommenced services on the loch after ceasing them in 1897. She was renamed *Lochshiel* shortly after entering service and, in 1962, was transferred to Iona to act as a tender to *King George V*, in which capacity she is seen here on 5 September 1969.

10 March 1955 saw the launch of the company's second *Claymore* by Denny of Dumbarton (QRC)

Claymore entered service on the Inner Islands mail route from Oban to Tobermory, Coll, Tiree, Castlebay, and Lochboisdale, which she maintained until 1971 and periodically until 1974. She is seen here at Kyle of Lochalsh when relieving *Loch Seaforth* for refit.

Claymore at Oban Railway Pier in 1971 with *King George V* at the site of the present linkspan.

Claymore inward bound for Oban in the sound of Mull with a flock of seagulls following her.

Claymore laid up at Greenock in 1974 with *King George V* behind her.

Claymore was sold in April 1976 to Greek owners and left the Clyde under the name *City of Andros*. She entered service considerably rebuilt for Cycladic Cruises under the name *City of Hydra* on the day excursion service from Flisvos Marina, east of the main port of Piraeus to Aegina, Poros and Hydra. She replaced *City of Piraeus* ex *Maid of Argyll* on this service and is seen here at Flisvos Marina in 1978.

City of Hydra approaching Piraeus in June 1988.

City of Hydra at Hydra in June 1990.

City of Hydra was withdrawn around 1993 and spent the next few years laid up at Eleusis, where she is seen in 1999. On 24 November 2000 she sank at her moorings. (BP).

Loch Ard was the final cargo ship to be built for the company, and came from Ferguson Bros. (Port Glasgow) Ltd in May 1955 and replaced *Hebrides*. She is seen here just after launching, still flying her builders' house flag. (QRC).

Loch Ard served initially on the Outer Islands cargo run from Glasgow, but moved to the Islay cargo service after 1964. She is seen here at Port Ellen in a postcard view.

MACBRAYNES STEAMERS

**WEEKLY
CARGO SAILINGS**

**FROM
GLASGOW**

AUGUST 1962 (Weather and circumstances permitting).
BY THE FOLLOWING OR OTHER STEAMERS.

STORNOWAY CARGO SERVICE   M.V. "LOCHDUNVEGAN"

LOADING BERTH - 8 KINGSTON DOCK   Tuesdays, 7th, 14th, 21st, 28th AUGUST.

Tobermory, Armadale (for Uig, Dunvegan, Carbost, Glenelg), Raasay, Portree, Stornoway, Tarbert (Harris).

ISLAY CARGO SERVICE   M.V. "LOCH ARD"

LOADING BERTH - 4 KINGSTON DOCK   Thursdays, 2nd, 9th, 16th, 23rd, 30th AUGUST.

Islay, Jura and Colonsay.   To Gigha. (via Port Ellen).

OUTER & INNER ISLANDS CARGO SERVICE   M.V. "LOCH CARRON"

LOADING BERTH - 6 KINGSTON DOCK   Fridays, 3rd, 10th, 17th, 24th, 31st AUGUST.

Salen, Coll, Tiree, Barra, Lochboisdale, Lochmaddy.

The order in which the Calls may be made is entirely at the discretion of the Masters of the Steamers, who will be guided by circumstances. Shippers should arrange with the undersigned as to Shipments, before actually sending down the Goods to the Sheds.

GOODS FOR LUING, LISMORE, *CROGGAN, CRAIGNURE, LOCHALINE, MINGARY, BUNESSAN, FIONPHORT, and IONA VIA TOBERMORY.
        FOR PORTNALONG, CARBOST, STRUAN, COLBOST, STEIN (WATERNISH), LOCHPOOLTEIL, DUNVEGAN, UIG, BROADFORD, ════ KYLEAKIN, EIGG, RHUM and CANNA VIA ARMADALE.
        FOR ERISKAY VIA LOCHBOISDALE.
        FOR LOCH SKIPPORT, KALLIN, FLODDA, GRIMSAY and LOCHEPORT VIA LOCHMADDY.
        FOR RODEL, FINSBAY, LEVERBURGH and SCALPAY VIA TARBERT (HARRIS).

GOODS SHOULD BE FULLY ADDRESSED TO THEIR FINAL DESTINATION.

*NOTE: CROGGAN SAILING OF 7th AUGUST ONLY.

DAVID MACBRAYNE LIMITED
44 ROBERTSON STREET, GLASGOW, C.2
TEL: CENTRAL 9231

JULY, 1962.

By 1962 only three MacBrayne cargo steamers remained in service, as seen in this cargo sailing bill for July 1962. (GEL).

Loch Toscaig had been built in 1945 as a Motor Fishing Vessel (MFV) named *Irene Julia*. She was purchased by MacBraynes in 1955 and operated from Kyle of Lochalsh to Toscaig to replace the Applecross calls previously made by the Stornoway mail steamer. She also operated short cruises from Kyle. From 1964 she served on the Oban to Lismore run and is seen here at Oban North Pier on 5 September 1969 with a MacBrayne bus in the background. She was sold in 1975 and used on sea angling trips from Gourock until wrecked in a storm in late 1978.

Ulva was built in 1956 for ferry services at Iona and Staffa. She survived in the fleet until the early months of 2001, latterly as the ferry at Eigg.

Loch Arkaig had been an inshore minesweeper of the MMS type and had been built by Bolson of Poole in 1942. She was purchased by MacBraynes in 1959 and entered service after conversion to passenger use in 1960. She initially replaced *Lochinvar* on the Mallaig-Kyle-Portree service and in 1964, with the withdrawal of the Outer Islands vessel from Mallaig, served the Small Isles of Eigg, Rhum, (as Rum was then spelled) and Canna. She is seen here leaving Mallaig.

From 1965 *Loch Arkaig* combined the Small Isles and Portree mail services, which she did until 1975 when the Portree service was withdrawn. She then offered the Small Isles service and, on certain days in the week, a Mallaig to Kyle run in summer with cruises from Kyle. In 1979 she sank in Mallaig harbour. She was raised, towed to Port Glasgow, and sold for use as a yacht. In 1980 she was sold again to Arab owners and was reported to have sunk off the coast of Spain. She is seen here at Mallaig along with the car ferry *Clansman*.

144

Loch Eynort was purchased in 1961 from the Commissioners of Irish Lights for whom she had served as the pilot boat *Valonia*. She had been built in 1947 by Wivenhoe Dockyard Ltd for Trinity House as a pilot cutter, and had been sold to Ireland in 1951. She sailed on the Kyle to Portree service from 1962 to 1964, and is seen here at Kyle. She saw little use after that, and was sold in 1971 for use as a yacht. (GEL).

Iona was another of the small red boats used to tender to *King George* V at Iona. Dickie of Tarbert built her in 1962 to replace her predecessor of the same name, which had been wrecked in a storm the previous year. She is seen here at Iona on 5 September 1969 with the Abbey in the background. She tendered at Staffa until 1965 and also served at Tobermory during the rebuilding of the pier in 1984-1985 and at Eigg, and was broken up in 1988.

Applecross had been built in 1944 as *Highlander* for Bruce Watt of Mallaig. She was purchased by MacBraynes in late 1963 and entered service the following year on the Kyle to Toscaig service, also offering a new mail sailing to Kylerhea three days a week. She is seen here beached at Tormore on Mull for hull repairs. (T. Faithful)

In 1965 *Applecross* went to Iona to join the fleet of small boats there and in 1969 she was sold to a Mr Gibson of Fionnphort, who operated the Fionnphort to Iona ferry service. This was taken over by Caledonian MacBrayne in 1973 around which time her cabin was removed. From 1981 she served on the Tobermory to Mingary route and was sold again to Mr Gibson in 1985. She is seen here arriving at Iona.

In 1964 three car ferries joined the fleet. These were built at Aberdeen by Hall Russell and were initially owned by the Secretary of State for Scotland, registered at Leith and chartered to David MacBrayne Ltd. The first to enter service was *Hebrides*. She started a new triangular route from Uig to Tarbert and Lochmaddy, and is seen here arriving at Tarbert after she had received CalMac funnel colours in 1973.

Hebrides at Gourock in spring 1981 when on the Clyde for overhaul. By now her port of registry had been changed to Glasgow.

Hebrides was sold in 1985 to Torbay Seaways for a service from Torquay to the Channel Islands for which she was renamed *Devoniun*. She served there from 1986 to 1991 and was sold again in 1993, renamed *Illyria* and ran from Italy to Albania for Illyria Lines but has latterly been laid up near Piraeus.

The second of the initial car ferry trio was *Clansman*. She initially operated from Mallaig to Armadale with, from 1971, an overnight service to Lochboisdale three nights a week. It will be seen that the new services offered by the *Hebrides* and *Clansman*, with connecting bus services, replaced the long Outer Isles service previously offered by the *Lochmor*. *Clansman* is seen her in a postcard view leaving Armadale.

In the winter and spring of 1970 *Clansman* was chartered to the Caledonian Steam Packet Co. for the Gurock to Dunoon run. She is seen here at Dunoon pier on 7 February 1970.

For this service her funnel was painted in the CSP colours of yellow with a black top. She is seen here at Dunoon on 23 May 1970 from *Maid of Ashton*.

In 1973 *Clansman* was lengthened and converted to a drive-through car ferry. In 1973 she served on the Ullapool to Stornoway service, but was then moved to the Ardrossan to Arran route, on which service she is seen here in September 1982.

Clansman arriving at Brodick in her rebuilt state. She was withdrawn in 1984 and sold to Maltese owners, being initially renamed *Tamira*, and then *Al Hussein*, and later *Al Rasheed*. She was placed in the Red Sea pilgrim trade and is now understood to be laid up.

Columba was the third of the trio to enter service. She ran from Oban to Craignure and Lochaline, but this was truncated to run to Craignure only, after the car ferry service was introduced between Lochaline and Fishnish. She maintained the Mull service until 1973. The hoist arrangement by which vehicles were loaded can be seen to advantage in this illustration.

Columba at Craignure. In the days of the *Lochinvar*, Craignure had been a ferry call, and the pier was only built in 1964.

Mini Cruises & Day Excursions from OBAN by r.m.s. Columba

From 1975 following the withdrawal of *King George V, Columba* was placed on the Iona run two days a week, serving Coll and Tiree on four days and Colonsay three times a week. By this time drive-through car ferries had taken over the Craignure run. Combinations of these sailings were offered as mini cruises.

Columba also offered special cruises for ship enthusiasts when she moved to Oban after overhaul in the spring in certain years. She is seen here at Gourock in 1979.

In her final season in 1988, *Columba* visited Tarbert (Loch Fyne), to celebrate the 100th anniversary of her illustrious forbear, on a special cruise en route from Gourock to Oban.

M.V. Hebridean Princess in Loch Duich 1990.

In that year she was sold and transformed to a luxury small cruise ship, named *Hebridean Princess*, entering service in 1989 and seen here in Loch Duich in 1990. Her cruises have mainly been in the western highlands and islands of Scotland, with occasional trips to the south of Ireland and to Norway.

Initially her car facilities were retained for passengers' cars, but at a later stage, as seen here, her lift was removed and the car deck converted to cabins. She has built a very loyal following in the years she has served as a cruise ship with more than 50% of her passenger being repeat business. The Berlitz Complete Guide to Cruising describes her as '*This utterly charming little ship has stately home service and a warm, totally cosseted, traditional country house ambience… one of the world's best kept travel secrets.*' She is seen here at Tarbert, Harris.

Hebridean Princess in the Mersey, at Liverpool on 9 November 1999, on her first visit there.

In November 1969, following the formation of the Scottish Transport Group, which owned both the CSP and MacBraynes, the CSP hoist-loading car ferry *Arran* of 1953 was transferred to the West Loch Tarbert to Islay service to replace the *Lochiel* and fill a long-felt need for a MacBrayne car ferry service to Islay, to compete with Western ferries' *Sound Of Islay*. She is seen here at the West Loch pier in 1970.

In 1972/1973 *Arran* was converted to a stern-loader as shown, Her lift was removed and the superstructure aft of this removed. She served Islay until the introduction of *Pioneer* in 1974. and is here leaving Gourock.

MacBraynes first drive through ship, and the last vessel to be ordered for David MacBrayne Ltd was the *Iona*, seen here fitting out at Troon in spring 1970. She had originally been designed for the Islay service, but plans for a new terminal had been aborted and her place had been taken by *Arran*. At this time she had a red black-topped funnel.

Iona, seen here off Ashton with Cowal in the background. She entered service on 29 May 1970 chartered to the CSP on the Dunoon service. A yellow black-topped CSP funnel replaced the red black-topped MacBrayne one after the first three days.

In 1972 her yellow funnel was repainted red and she operated on the Mallaig to Kyle and Stornoway service. Seen in 1973 whilst operating the Mull service.

In winter 1974-1975 she had additional passenger cabins fitted on the bridge deck in place of the dummy funnel. Her exhaust uptakes were heightened and were painted as her new funnels. At this time she was on the service from Oban to Castlebay and Lochboisdale and is seen here at Lochaline in 1975.

In 1979 *Iona* took up the Islay run, the route she was built for ten years earlier, which now commenced at the former Western Ferries terminal at Kennacraig rather than West Loch Tarbert as previously. She is seen here off Port Ellen.

With the arrival of the *Isle of Arran* on the Islay service in 1993, *Iona* moved to a new roll on-roll off Mallaig to Armadale summer service and served as general relief ship in the winter months. She is seen here at Armadale Pier before te addition of a Linkspan.

Iona in August 1997 leaving Mallaig for Armadale.

In November 1997, *Iona* was withdrawn and sold to Pentland Ferries of Orkney. This was a new operator who hoped to establish a new service from St Margaret's Hope to Gills Bay near John O'Groats. *Iona* was renamed *Pentalina B*, but saw no service on this route until May 2001. She was chartered back to Caledonian MacBrayne in May 1998 for a short spell and is seen here arriving at Oban on 4 May of that year in that guise.

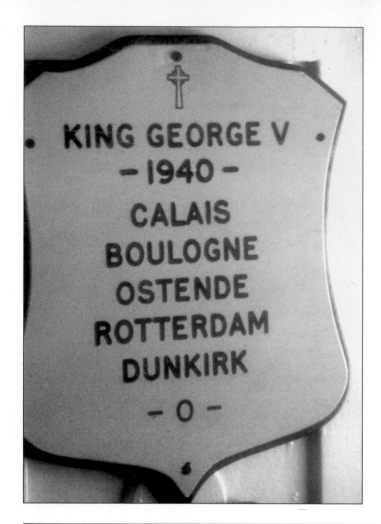

KING GEORGE V
- 1940 -
CALAIS
BOULOGNE
OSTENDE
ROTTERDAM
DUNKIRK
- O -

One of several war service plaques which were on board *King George* V. The one illustrated is currently on display on Clyde Marine Services *Kenilworth,* which operates from Gourock to Kilcreggan and Helensburgh. This was donated by Andrew Lindsay, who founded the West Highland Steamer Club in 1967